The New York Times

THINK OUTSIDE THE BOX CROSSWORDS
Witty, Wild Wordplay

Edited by Will Shortz

ST. MARTIN'S GRIFFIN ❧ NEW YORK

THE NEW YORK TIMES THINK OUTSIDE THE BOX CROSSWORDS.
Copyright © 2008 by The New York Times Company. All rights reserved.
Printed in the United States of America. For information, address
St. Martin's Press, 175 Fifth Avenue, New York, N.Y. 10010.

www.stmartins.com

All of the puzzles that appear in this work were originally published
in *The New York Times* from January 16, 2001, to January 31, 2008.
Copyright © 2001, 2002, 2003, 2004, 2005, 2006, 2007, 2008 by
The New York Times Company.
All rights reserved. Reprinted by permission.

ISBN-13: 978-0-312-38261-2
ISBN-10: 0-312-38261-8

First Edition: July 2008

10 9 8 7 6 5 4 3 2 1

The New York Times

THINK OUTSIDE THE BOX CROSSWORDS

ACROSS

1 Punching tool
4 Minus
8 Purity units
14 "Quiet down!"
15 Lie next to
16 Supreme Egyptian god
17 Summer weather phenomenon
19 Dreadlocks wearers
20 With little effort
21 Itinerary word
23 Nervous twitches
24 Like an old cigar
25 Repel, as an attack
27 25-Down, e.g.
29 Within view
30 Marina event
35 Drum majors' props
39 Basin accompanier
40 Coeur d'___, Idaho
42 Feminine suffix
43 Arnaz and Ball's studio
45 Eat quickly
47 Pick up
49 Bering, e.g.: Abbr.
50 Dark, heavy type
53 A black key
58 Colombian city
59 Bruised item, maybe
60 Automat, e.g.
61 Ersatz gold
63 Winter weather phenomenon
65 Launderer, at times
66 Sheriff Taylor's son
67 Former New York City mayor Beame
68 Admits, with "up"
69 Not very much
70 Part of CBS: Abbr.

DOWN

1 Hibachi residue
2 Toast choice
3 Tibet's capital
4 Like the Wild West
5 Popular site for collectors
6 Ford Explorer, e.g.: Abbr.
7 Martin of "Roxanne"
8 Martial arts wear
9 "I ___ Rock" (1966 hit)
10 Went back to the top
11 Bit of silliness
12 CD segment
13 Get snippy with
18 Up to, briefly
22 Actor Holm
25 High school subj.
26 Ovine utterance
28 Some prom night drivers
30 Hospital unit
31 Have markers out
32 Loser to D.D.E.
33 Lots and lots and lots
34 A browser browses it, with "the"
36 Lennon's lady
37 Compass heading
38 Six-yr. term holder
41 It smells
44 Topper
46 Like most tires
48 Baseball put-out
50 Ballet rail
51 "Stand and Deliver" star
52 Après-ski drink
54 McHenry and Sumter: Abbr.
55 Olin and Horne
56 Sheikdom of song
57 Pounds on an Underwood
58 Salon creation
60 Director Kazan
62 Jackie Onassis' sister
64 Make a choice

The circled letters will show a "change in the weather."

by Eric Berlin

2

ACROSS
1 Sports column?
5 Standard deviation symbol
10 War fare?
14 Like many a hurricane
15 Allege in defense
16 Coat or skirt preceder
17 Disappointing election results
19 Seasoned
20 Help
21 Equal
22 Channeled
23 Resolute advice to the hesitant
27 Stuff for surfacing
28 He painted clocks
29 Community contest
30 Stumpers?
33 Flags
34 Hal Foster comic character
35 One associated with honesty
36 No one special
38 Castilian hero
39 Expert on the rules
40 Good relations
41 Manages, with "out"
42 N.Y. minutes?
43 Fountain in New Orleans
44 Word for word: Abbr.
46 1985 sequel to a classic 1939 film
48 Donny or Marie Osmond, e.g.
51 Unit of nautical displacement
52 Tall topper
54 Gee
56 Like bats
58 Biblical book
59 Available
60 Small animal shelter
61 Short time out?
62 They follow cuts
63 Dict. offering

DOWN
1 First name in animation
2 "This ___ Youth" (Kenneth Lonergan play)
3 Just learning about
4 Discovery of Galileo
5 Comparatively quick
6 Long series of woes
7 Lee, e.g.: Abbr.
8 ___ wheel
9 Plugs
10 Burn
11 Gripping read
12 Brutally destroy
13 Season opener?
18 Miss, south of the border
21 Parsley relative
23 Fine accompaniment?
24 Promise, e.g.
25 À la Poe
26 Fractures
28 Exile of 1302
30 Kitchen gizmo
31 Really big
32 Rights shouldn't be taken from it
33 Frosty
36 No performers are found here
37 Red sky, maybe
41 Colorize, e.g.
44 Immerses
45 Draper's unit
47 Cad
48 Slight indication?
49 "What ___!" ("Hilarious!")
50 Like some habits
52 Numerical prefix
53 Overflow
54 Modicum
55 Insurance letters
56 Green-light indicator
57 Person

by James M. Jenista and James C. Jenista

3

ACROSS

1 A lap a minute, e.g.
5 Graceful bend
9 Capital south of Quito
13 Norse saint
14 "___ She Sweet"
15 Quotation notation
16 Leather finish?
17 Jump the gun
19 Generally ignored astronomical occurrence
21 Token takers
22 "Piece of cake!"
24 One's partner
25 Reebok rival
27 Cartoonist Peter
29 Short break?
30 Genealogist's work
31 PC innards: Abbr.
34 "Concord" Sonata composer
35 Flip response?
36 Whispers sweet nothings
37 Fine points
38 "Okey-doke"
39 Puts out some hot, swinging music
40 Manilow song setting
41 Gasbag
42 Unwelcome guest
44 Marsh plants
46 Took a look inside
48 Wood cutters
51 Exact heavy vengeance
53 Poi party
54 Quick points
55 One often asked for an autograph
56 Outlet option
57 E-mailed
58 Writes
59 Work unit

DOWN

1 Elegy, e.g.
2 Chorus girl
3 Tough mode of punishment
4 50-50 chance
5 On-call gizmos
6 Purposely misinform
7 I.R.A. increaser: Abbr.
8 Greek vowels
9 Bodega patron
10 Together
11 Amusing Amsterdam
12 Them, in "Them!"
18 Epitaph holder . . . or Mick Jagger?
20 Have words (with)
23 Ballet support
25 Wanting water
26 Humorist Barry
28 Sells to the public
30 Bar mitzvah reading
31 Where shrimp take a dip
32 Elbow
33 Cold war inits.
35 "Careful!"
36 Picnic dish
38 Bad losers
39 Blacksmith's file
40 Coquettish in the extreme
41 Singing sounds
42 Gird (oneself)
43 Solid, as some furniture
45 Sweater synthetic
46 Brief holiday?
47 Tap trouble
49 Go in up to one's ankles
50 Use a straw
52 Laudatory lines

by Nancy Salomon and Harvey Estes

4

ACROSS

1 Underworld figure
5 Return
10 Without thinking
14 Fire __
15 It sticks in the kitchen
16 Class of '98 member, e.g.
17 Join
18 Bottle in the bathroom
19 Sight on much old Roman statuary
20 Fierce military action
22 "Yikes!"
23 Cries of pain
24 Headache
26 Tribal V.I.P.
30 Dry with absorbent paper
32 Paint choice
33 1967 film set in a prison camp
38 Dollar competitor
39 Bandleader Shaw
40 Jet black
41 Begin to understand
43 Surgical opening?
44 Holly
45 Star of 33-Across
46 City south of Yosemite
50 Rev.'s talk
51 Dancing girl in "The Return of the Jedi"
52 Collaborated
59 Path
60 Grant-__
61 Certain horses
62 James of jazz
63 Ancient Greek festival site
64 Prefix with biology
65 Basic telephone

66 Welcome
67 Continue

DOWN

1 Herder
2 Peeved, after "in"
3 Texas's __ Duro Canyon
4 Veteran
5 Overwhelmingly
6 Malt liquor foams
7 Riyadh native
8 Site of Jesus' first miracle
9 Tough spot
10 "A Garden of Earthly Delights" novelist
11 Thrashes
12 Like some Bach works
13 Individually crafted

21 Gently persuade
25 Nearby
26 Remains at a steel mill
27 Suffer from
28 Bickering
29 __ Verde
30 Modern injection
31 Order at a butcher's
33 Saskatchewan tribe
34 Early movie mogul
35 Coin word
36 Actress Sedgwick
37 Former Nebraska senator James
39 Granting
42 Submit
43 Square
45 "Can I help?"
46 Open shot

47 Origin
48 Lift the spirits of
49 1978 Peace Nobelist
50 Did telemarks, e.g.
53 Scott Turow book
54 "__ Lama Ding Dong" (1961 hit)
55 Place for keys and lipstick
56 "Othello" villain
57 Laura who wrote "Wedding Bell Blues"
58 Personal and direct

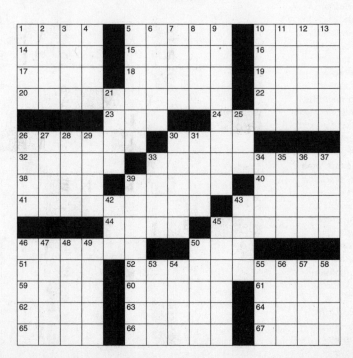

by Alan Arbesfeld

ACROSS

1 Second in a series
5 Ship to remember
10 Saudi citizen
14 Singular person
15 Spirit
16 Showroom sample
17 S
20 Squab alternative
21 Shortstop of fame
22 Significant period
23 Started moving
27 Sea or way ending
29 Screenwriter James
30 Sister of Thalia
31 Sexy person
37 Scream or be rowdy, as a child
38 Strapped
39 Signature tune
44 Spill consequence
45 Solo for Renata Scotto
46 Sort of cuisine
47 Snaps again
52 Select
53 Skirt style
54 Schaffhausen's river
57 's
63 Sporting blade
64 Stockpile
65 Scoreboard postings
66 Series of legis. meetings
67 See eye to eye
68 Sour fruit

DOWN

1 Seckel's cousin
2 Single-named singer
3 Soothing, weatherwise
4 Site where trees are displayed
5 Start to function?
6 Sandy's sound
7 Swearing-in words
8 Scand. land
9 Sounds of hesitation
10 Stella who founded an acting conservatory
11 Send for information
12 Slay, in a way
13 Sick and tired
18 Soap may be found like this
19 Spoon-bender Geller
23 Scrooge's cry
24 Sense of self
25 Salon offering
26 Scale's top, sometimes
27 Skillful act
28 St. Louis sight
32 Still woolly
33 Similes' relatives
34 Stunning
35 Shorten, in a way
36 Sandberg of baseball
40 Stood no more
41 Smeltery input
42 "Seduction of the Minotaur" author
43 Station ration
47 Sprints
48 Split to unite
49 Speeders' penalties
50 Stud fees
51 Sun. talk
55 Spanish boy
56 Seneca's being
58 "So that's it!"
59 Slot filler in a gearwheel
60 Seaman
61 Spleen
62 Shelley work

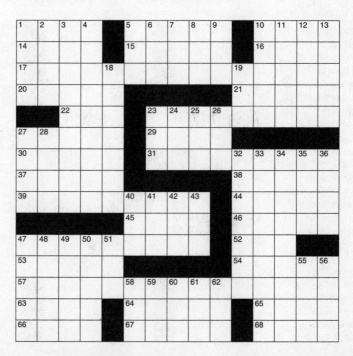

by Richard Silvestri

6

ACROSS
1 Crown
5 Store
10 Spout nonsense?
14 Bird in a bevy
15 DuPont's "Fiber A"
16 Cass, e.g.
17 Biblical verb
18 Roller-coaster parts
19 Brand under a sink
20 ___ Lindgren, creator of Pippi Longstocking
22 Unwelcome strains
24 Action film staple
25 Popular show
28 Way off base?
29 Robert Burns's "O, ___ Thou in the Cauld Blast"
30 Inn order
32 Formicary resident
34 Like some kitchens
38 The show's partly completed puzzle (category: hosts)
43 Old Ford
44 ___ Paulo
45 Shorten, in a way
46 Subtracting
49 "I'm innocent!"
52 Request that will complete the show's puzzle
57 Compound ending
58 Impending
59 Traveler's complaint
60 Interrogate
62 Place for a French lesson
64 Powder holder
65 Motivation
66 Issue
67 First word of "The Raven"
68 With 40-Down, popular fashion label
69 Clean, as a floor
70 Appt. with an analyst

DOWN
1 "Stop yer joshin'!"
2 Soaked
3 Kitschy
4 Part of an order
5 Soft leather
6 Coach Parseghian
7 Bluff
8 Like jack-o'-lanterns
9 Protect
10 Wee, in the Hebrides
11 Spicy cuisine
12 Floor
13 Kind of stand
21 Pier grp.
23 Scatter
26 Manage
27 The Beehive State
30 Lug
31 Old Ford
33 DVD displayers
35 Soul searcher's need
36 L.A. law figure
37 Modernized
39 Set
40 See 68-Across
41 Prefix with technology
42 What money is to some
47 Clay targets
48 Placid Everglades denizen
50 Calendar abbr.
51 Underlying system of beliefs
52 Bury
53 See fit
54 Figure of speech
55 Ones who make raids
56 Moorehead of "Bewitched"
57 Soothing shade
61 Last in a series
63 Fat ___ (fight memento)

by Patrick Merrell

ACROSS

1 Often-told truths
5 ___ facto
9 Tricky shot
14 Racer Luyendyk
15 Gardener's purchase
16 Some saxes
17 Lava geese
18 It's passed on
19 Contents of some John Cage compositions
20 Start of a question
23 Adjusts
24 Big ___
25 Whomps, briefly
28 Old Mideast combine: Abbr.
29 John Dean, to Nixon
32 Sure way to lose money
34 "Gosh!"
35 Ruined
37 A star may have one
38 Middle of the question
41 Place
43 Discernment
44 Common ratio
46 Sample
50 Chamber piece?
49 Dispatched
51 Monk's title
52 Driver's aid: Abbr.
54 Track racer
56 End of the question
60 Like workhorses
62 Arcade name
63 V.I.P.'s opposite
64 It's passed on
65 Compelled
66 Wading bird

67 Ottawa-born singer/songwriter
68 Turned up
69 Cry that might be appropriate at this point in the puzzle

ACROSS

1 Retreat
2 Passage between buildings
3 Bingo announcement
4 "Toodles!"
5 Mirage
6 Magician's sound effect
7 Draped dress
8 Things to be read
9 Om, e.g.
10 Cream ingredient
11 Malodorous pest
12 Coded message

13 Language suffix often seen in crosswords
13 Compass dir. often seen in crosswords
21 African grazer
22 Put words in someone's mouth?
26 Anthem contraction
27 Platform place: Abbr.
30 Is hip to
31 1995 country hit "Someone ___ Star"
33 "Dagnabbit!"
35 Latched
36 Affectedly dainty, in England
37 Extinct Namibian shrub genus: Var.

38 Coordinated effort
39 Like some seats
40 First
41 Trip producer
42 W.W. II Pacific battle site, for short
44 Appropriate
45 Blazing
47 Cat
48 Desired response to "Take my wife . . . please!"
50 Open-sided shelter
53 Perfume source
55 Noted archer
57 What a germ may become
58 Good sign
59 Ticks off
60 Hearst kidnapping grp.
61 Dear

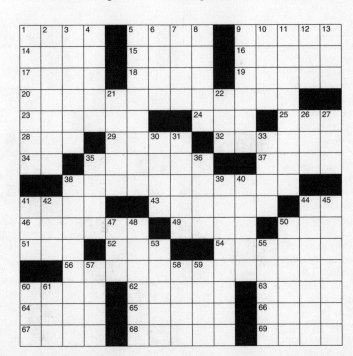

by Patrick Merrell

The circled letters in the answers to the seven starred clues, reading left to right or top to bottom, spell words that can complete familiar phrases that start with "break."

ACROSS

1 Throw
5 It may be found in a cone
9 Homes for mil. planes
13 Object of a manhunt, maybe
14 Score just before winning
15 Skylit courts
16 *Not just stupid
18 Where William the Conqueror died
19 Kerosene
20 N.B.A. center who has pitched for McDonald's, Pepsi and Visa
22 *Setting in Sherlock Holmes's "The Man With the Twisted Lip"
24 The hots
25 Snow ___
26 Les Trois Mousquetaires, e.g.
28 Strain
31 "Eat at ___"
34 Shopaholic's delight
35 Canyon part
36 Daily or weekly, e.g.: Abbr.
37 *Perplexed state
39 1970s polit. cause
40 Early sixth-century year
41 Partner of aids
42 Come clean, with "up"
43 Slippery swimmer
44 "The ___ Report," 1976 best seller
45 Co. with a triangular logo
47 Grill
49 *Informers
54 Seven Sisters grads
57 Major Italian tourist site
58 "Ich ___ dich" (German words of endearment)
59 *Dessert made from a product of a 10-Down
61 Satyric looks
62 Sleeper ___
63 This and that
64 "Finnegans Wake" wife
65 Major rtes.
66 Ivy League school in Philly

DOWN

1 Cellist Casals
2 "That's ___!" (director's cry)
3 "Ditto"
4 Blunders
5 "Well, ___!"
6 ___ Hugo, 1975 Isabelle Adjani role based on a real-life story
7 Through
8 Granatelli of auto racing
9 Bits
10 *Orchard part
11 "Très ___"
12 Did a number
15 Stimulated
17 1890s gold rush city
21 Completely strange
23 Music download source
27 They replaced C rations
29 Pretense
30 Short holiday?
31 Shade of green
32 Garfield's housemate
33 *Fairy tale meanie
34 Put back in
37 Some luau dancers
38 Resort island ESE of Valencia
42 Cigarette box feature
45 Ocean rings
46 "How foolish ___!"
48 Planetary shadow
50 Be in force, as a rule
51 Author Zora ___ Hurston
52 Popular Japanese beer
53 Squelch
54 Milan's Teatro ___ Scala
55 Collateral option
56 Individually
60 Church perch

by Paula Gamache

ACROSS

1 Clear of stale odors, maybe
7 Early Ford
13 Catastrophic
15 Genetic shapes
16 Dracula's least favorite citations?
18 Asian occasion
19 Tiny bit
20 "Well, ___ had it!"
21 Swedish-based furniture chain
23 Cozy inn, briefly
25 Puts to work
26 Historian Thomas who wrote "The French Revolution"
28 Drifting
30 1950 film noir classic
31 ___-X
32 Dracula's least favorite sporting event?
41 Grand Cherokee, e.g.: Abbr.
42 Ink dispenser?
43 Night school subj.
44 Sound at a salon
46 Lascivious sort
47 It merged with Mattel in 1997
48 "Pale" drinks
50 Actress Sorvino
51 Staggering
52 Maple product
55 Director Kurosawa
57 Dracula's least favorite time?
60 Unreturnable serve
61 Golf reservation
62 Elephant grp.
63 Kind of school
64 Doesn't fold
65 Aves.

DOWN

1 Frigid
2 California's motto
3 One who's revolting?
4 Reply to a ques.
5 How-___ (handy books)
6 Prefix with Asian
7 French sea
8 Rousing cheer
9 Kipling's "Gunga ___"
10 Cut out
11 "Frasier" actress Jane
12 Size up
14 Hairs on a caterpillar
15 Ibsen's "___ Gabler"
17 Idol follower
22 Robert of Broadway's "Guys and Dolls"
23 White wines
24 Sequel to Kerouac's "On the Road"
25 One out on a limb?
27 John left Cynthia for her
29 "Miracle" team of 1969
32 Ltr. additions
33 Compete in track
34 Having a mean, mean look
35 Pilot's prediction: Abbr.
36 Tosspot
37 007, for one
38 Janitor's belt attachments
39 Snail at Chez Jacques
40 Warning in a school zone
45 Stage after a sunburn
47 Disneyland's Enchanted ___ Room
49 Narrow cuts
50 Whiz
51 Comic Sandler
52 Home to the 29-Down
53 Trial fig.
54 Trident-shaped letters
56 Nile snakes
58 Pick up
59 French friend

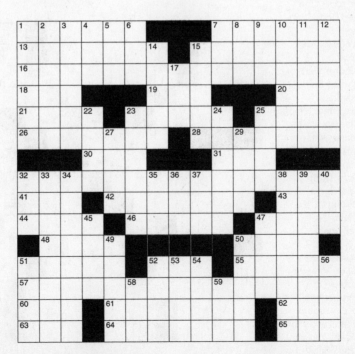

by Patrick Blindauer

10

Twelve answers in this puzzle are to be entered in an unusual way, for you to discover.

ACROSS

1 E.R. amts.
4 Geographical name that means roughly "great land"
10 "An Essay on Criticism" essayist
14 Leftover bit
15 Reading of 98.6°, e.g.
16 Casual footwear
17 First-rate
18 Singles' world
20 Pre-Red head
22 Tiny complaints
23 Oklahoma tribe
24 Moving
26 Tries
28 Lap dog
30 Kind of radio
34 Alphabet trio
37 Stalled construction
38 For some time
40 Peter Cottontail's pace
42 Ella Fitzgerald classic
43 Station rating
44 Speaker in the outfield
45 Shropshire female
46 Some Joe Frazier wins
47 Irons
50 Drang's partner
51 Yellow parts
55 Cause for a blessing?
59 Hike
61 A millionth of a milli-
62 Nickel-nursers
65 Not go straight
66 Rabble
67 Phone button
68 Hosp. readout
69 Cards traded for Musials, maybe
70 Burly
71 Blue hue

DOWN

1 White vestment
2 Traverse back and forth
3 Annual parade honoree, briefly
4 Clause joiner
5 Museum deal
6 Craftsmanship
7 Lovestruck
8 Part of the Louisiana Purchase
9 H.S. subj.
10 Sgt.'s charges
11 Olive genus
12 Rec room activity
13 It involves a wave of the hand
19 Terse radio message
21 Basket feature
25 Six-Day War figure
27 "Out!"
29 Trendy
30 Spa sounds
31 Stand-up's prop
32 Zoomed
33 Parcel (out)
34 Kerflooey
35 Pendulum accompaniment
36 Capable of
39 Spineless
41 ___ de deux
42 Perfumed
44 House mover?
48 Old arm
49 Roughly one of every two deliveries
50 Pacifier
52 Lolls
53 Trinket
54 Damp
55 Prefix with phobia
56 Small talk
57 Importance
58 Galoots
60 Scaler's goal
63 Yearbook sect.
64 Wily

by Patrick Merrell

ACROSS

1 Like a melon
6 Be itinerant
10 One who's driving on air?
14 Top mark
15 Book before Nehemiah
16 Take on
17 Telephone the catalog merchant Bean at midnight?
19 Census data
20 Record label known for compilations
21 Pencil holder, at times
22 President-___
23 Physics unit
24 Select a 1918 Billy Murray song?
27 Chinese restaurant flower
29 Fix
30 Costa del ___
31 Baseball's Bud
32 Succor
33 Brontë heroine
34 Fast jets for a top banana?
38 Velvety growth
41 Sch. group
42 Cummerbund's place
46 Wrath
47 All-Star third baseman Ron
48 Gripes
50 Half a dozen erotic pictures of chests?
53 "The Bells" poet
54 Wreck
55 Hall-of-Famer nicknamed "Bobby Hockey"
56 Mark on a graph
57 "The Black Stallion" boy
58 Commercials for a Des Moines driving org.?
61 "Etta ___"
62 Raised
63 Neither early nor late
64 Little Oil Drop was its mascot
65 Statistics figure
66 Stays fresh

DOWN

1 Hardcover covers
2 Trapped
3 Criminal
4 Select
5 Fashion inits.
6 Tie the knot a second time?
7 Arkansas's ___ Mountains
8 College major
9 Madonna's role in "A League of Their Own"
10 Pool hall need
11 New Orleans, with "the"
12 Builder
13 Change the look of
18 Luau souvenirs
22 Heart chart: Abbr.
24 Comics possum
25 Rap's ___ Kross
26 Grade-schoolers
28 Barbecue fare
32 Simile center
33 Actor Morales
35 Glasses, commercially
36 Charon's river
37 "___ the night . . ."
38 Boner
39 Ripken's team for 3,001 games
40 Ice hockey teams, e.g.
43 One way to jog
44 Arose
45 Flies over the equator?
47 First year in St. Pius I's papacy
48 Thanksgiving Day event
49 Vega's constellation
51 Brand of knife
52 Participated in crew
56 Glazier's item
58 PC maker, once
59 Guadalajara gold
60 Fine, informally

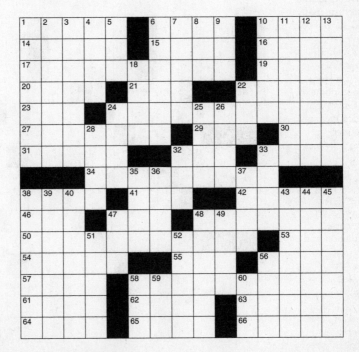

by Peter Gordon

12

Sixteen answers in this puzzle have something unusual in common. What is it?

ACROSS
1 Pequod captain
5 Immense
9 Footnote abbr.
13 End of many '60s dance club names
14 Cupid
15 Bridge site
16 Sticky
17 Disgusted response
18 Did horribly on, as a test
19 "You __ here"
20 French yeses
22 "Nerts!"
24 Lazy one, slangily
26 Make unclear
27 Trifle (with)
28 Chinese drink
32 1948 also-ran
35 Talks raucously
36 Mound builder
37 Plaintive woodwind
38 One of 18 French kings
39 Good name for a Dalmatian
40 Place for a plug
41 Courted
42 Like saltwater taffy
43 Orchestral performance
45 Any ship
46 Frenchman Descartes
47 Hamilton and Burr did it
51 Cuckoo
54 Seethe
55 Eggs
56 1997 title role for Peter Fonda
57 Hazard warning
59 Farm call
61 Welsh form of John
62 Hero
63 Moran and Brockovich
64 Puppy sounds
65 Slangy denial
66 "Not on __!"

DOWN
1 Ancient market
2 Nonsense
3 ID info
4 "Hot-diggity-dog!"
5 Flavorless
6 Quantities: Abbr.
7 Exemplar of little worth
8 Delivery room surprise?
9 Natural
10 __ tie
11 "Ah, yes"
12 Like a lawn at dawn
13 1946 hit "__ in Calico"
21 180° turn, slangily
23 Tints
25 To __ (exactly)
26 Pigtail, e.g.
28 Causing to stick
29 Item for a D.J.
30 Sufficient, once
31 Lawyer: Abbr.
32 Executes
33 Web auction site
34 Bird's find
35 Pat or Daniel
38 Place of wildness, informally
39 Author Silverstein
41 "Thank heaven that's over!"
42 Onetime White House daughter
44 Primps
45 __ generis
47 Last name in mysteries
48 Sarge's superior
49 Happening
50 During working hours
51 Chop __
52 Ovid's 156
53 Bring in the sheaves
54 Betty __
58 Japanese vegetable
60 Sphere

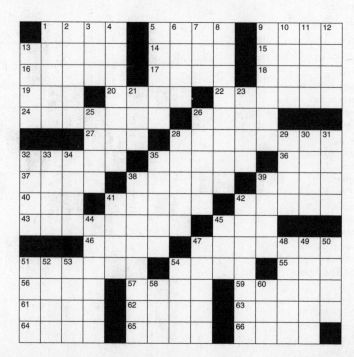

by Susan Harrington Smith

ACROSS

1 Leading lady
5 It's said when taking off
9 Take off
14 Kaffiyeh sporter
15 Score after deuce
16 People concerned with feet
17 President Taft's alma mater
18 It may be driven during a storm
19 Namely
20 Like a line
23 Coll. hoops competition
24 Beam
25 Place for a shore dinner, maybe
29 Height enhancer
31 "Listen, ___ . . ."
34 "The Brady Bunch" housekeeper
35 Self-starter?
36 Ear piece
37 They're packed during the holidays
40 Suffix for high-tech gadgets
41 Groundless
42 Take forcefully
43 Teutonic name part
44 Don't take off
45 Sky pilots, so to speak
46 Animal with a mane
47 Hegelian article
48 Hit Broadway play of 1945, with "The"
55 Walk together
57 ___ end
58 Major gold-mining area, with "the"
59 Certain backwater
60 Member of an instrument family
61 Fizzy wine, familiarly
62 59-Across relative
63 Wax makers
64 One that gets tongue-tied?

DOWN

1 Harry Belafonte catchword
2 Home of many mullahs
3 Hollow between hills
4 Not up yet
5 State adjoining the Bass Strait
6 Unlikely to reconsider
7 Pantry containers
8 "___ quote . . ."
9 Like some injuries
10 Now
11 Whirl
12 Possessive pronoun
13 Hrs. in the West
21 Private
22 Lunchbox treats
25 Show with skits
26 Olds model
27 Really tease
28 Self-confident assertion
29 By any practical means
30 Ranch add-on?
31 More tender
32 Past plump
33 Egg holders
35 Heather's "Melrose Place" role
36 Powerful person
38 Shakespeare's Andronicus
39 Nashville sound?
44 Buy in a hurry
45 "Grand" things
46 Opposite of cheer
47 Spring (from)
48 Maja painter
49 General Motors division
50 Famed "7" wearer
51 Times to remember
52 Ill-considered
53 Turned on by
54 Falco of "The Sopranos"
55 Cable's Superstation
56 Like some deals

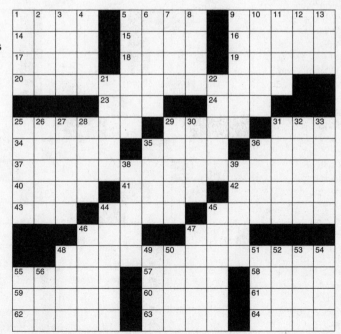

by Dan Reichert

14

ACROSS

1 ___ d'Ouessant (westernmost point of France)
4 Greek director Angelopoulos
8 '60s TV boy
12 Piatigorsky specialty
15 Place for portraits
16 Thin haze
17 At full throttle
18 Put in ___ for
19 Friend of the powerless: Abbr.
20 Changed but not seriously
22 Stops: Abbr.
23 Win over
24 Support
26 Scientology founder ___ Hubbard
28 Battlements in Spanish castles
30 Not straight
33 Ran into
35 Pocket
36 Org. for arguers?
37 "Attention!"
40 Part of a metaphor
41 Rich boy in "Nancy"
43 Heat source
44 Particular
45 It may smooth the way
47 More than "Phooey!"
49 Strong
52 The house of Juan Carlos
56 Region NW of Genoa
57 Hurricane Carter, for one
59 End of a punch?
60 Leg up
61 Certain fur
62 It has many hitches
63 Many an old Hapsburg subject
64 Nero's land
65 Horace volume
66 Deli order
67 Travel method

DOWN

1 Start of an old boast
2 Bar wedge
3 Animal with a black stripe down its back
4 Spring event
5 1980s Mideast envoy Philip
6 Exclusive
7 Routine
8 In some way
9 Tip to solving this puzzle (with the key parts to be said out loud)
10 Fidgety, maybe
11 Pests to Australian ranchers
13 Apt
14 Two semesters
21 ___ One (indoor kart racing)
25 Founding editor of The New Yorker
27 Just out
29 Lambaste
30 At ___ speed (quickly)
31 Like poll taxes
32 This puzzle, e.g.
34 Music, dance, painting, etc.
37 Find (out)
38 1963 title role for Paul Newman
39 Together
42 Demographer's grouping
44 Egg on
46 Tangle
48 Famous blonde bombshell
50 Move furtively
51 Hoover's predecessor?
53 Ancient marketplace
54 Actress Belafonte
55 ___ of roses
56 Prefix with phobia
58 Rock group from Akron that was a 1980 one-hit wonder

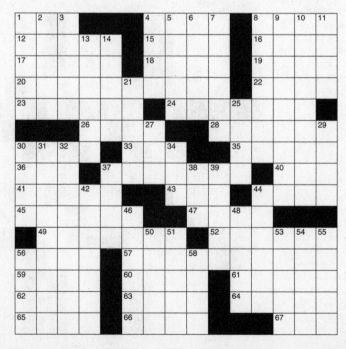

by M. Francis Vuolo

ACROSS

1 Airborne toy
6 "The Simpsons" storekeeper
9 Loafers holder
14 Après-ski drink
15 Zip
16 Spacious
17 Native on the Bering Sea
18 Sea lion, e.g.
20 Horseshoer's tool
21 Sports page summary
22 Purge
23 Sinuous swimmer
25 Galley tool
26 Fall off
27 Like the verb "to be"
31 Bigot
32 Society page word
33 "Step ___!"
34 Bamako's land
35 Theater receipts
37 It shouldn't be stuffed
40 Boozehound
41 Smidgens
42 Dundee denial
43 French seaport
45 Food device
47 10K, for one
48 "You stink!"
49 Triangle part: Abbr.
50 CPR giver
51 Tune player
53 Scads
57 "Come to think of it . . ."
59 A-1
60 Pitchfork wielder
61 Actor Billy ___ Williams
62 Emerson piece
63 Excellent viewing spot
64 Comics bark
65 Transmission

DOWN

1 Part of a freight train
2 ___ nut (caffeine source)
3 Boardwalk treats
4 False top
5 Chow down
6 Zoo animals
7 Naval attire
8 Commotion
9 One-named singer from Nigeria
10 Pinafore letters
11 Organ transplants, e.g.
12 "Seinfeld" pal
13 Tree of the maple family
19 Blunder
21 Meal-to-go
24 Self-interested one
26 Mural site
27 Correspondence collector
28 Antique auto
29 Like a mirror
30 Get prone
31 W.W. II U.S. admiral nicknamed "Bull"
34 Miniature auto brand
36 It may be blown
37 Life story, in brief
38 Chinese "path"
39 Filmdom's Rocky, e.g.
41 Range part
43 Classic item in size comparisons
44 Any of several Egyptian kings
45 Spanish inn
46 Meager
48 Florida N.F.L.er
51 Become soft
52 Staff leader
54 Actress Kudrow
55 Mullah ___, former Afghan leader
56 Place for playthings
58 River inlet
59 Hard throw, in baseball

by Ron O'Hair

16

ACROSS

1 ___-Deutschland
4 Quaff with caramel coloring
9 Locks holder
14 Just scratch the surface?
15 Skip ___
16 Shaded house parts
17 Comers
19 Iroquoian Indians
20 Modern highway sights, for short
22 ___ flu
23 "The Tower" poet
24 Guitarist Lofgren
27 "77 Sunset Strip" character
31 Writes
36 It makes men mean
37 Golden State postgrads, for short
40 Rd. way
41 Giddiness
42 Like a prom
45 Russian river
46 Kind of acid in olive oil
49 Calculator brand
53 Popular family room appliances, for short
57 Opposite of neo-
58 Like Parliament
59 Circle
60 Sensory input
61 Prefix with color
62 Brooklyn's ___ Institute, college of art and architecture
63 Teaspoonsful, often
64 "Holy smokes!"

DOWN

1 Horseshoe-shaped symbol
2 Actress Emma of "Dynasty"
3 Rome's Fontana di ___
4 Primitive practice
5 "___ Holden," Irving Bacheller novel
6 Hang
7 Did nothing
8 "Who's there?" response
9 Looks after
10 Famed tenor
11 Part of a city name that means "spring" in Hebrew
12 Pinky and Spike
13 Some afterthoughts, in brief
18 Country with a Hutu majority
21 Rooster, for some
25 Office gizmo
26 Treats, in adspeak
28 Longtime sportswriter Roger
29 Where to find Pennsylvania Ave.
30 Leisure
31 Hang ten, e.g.
32 Prefix with plasm
33 Card or Met
34 Big Midwest sch.
35 Popular fragrance
38 Euros replaced them
39 George E. ___, 1974 Medicine Nobelist
43 "Go, go, go!"
44 "Little Men" author
47 Misbehaves
48 Yasir Arafat's birthplace
50 Tickle, as strings
51 Mrs. Trump, once
52 Singer K. T. ___
53 She had a "Tootsie" role
54 Isle of exile
55 Three-stripers, e.g.: Abbr.
56 British title
57 Dad

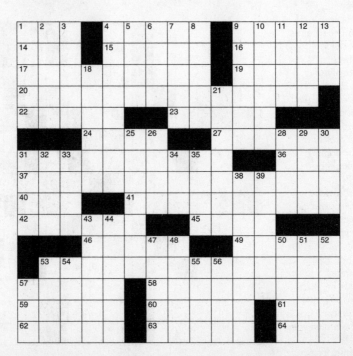

by Patrick Merrell

ACROSS

1 Contest official
6 Smart
11 Pavement caution
14 "___ to recall . . ."
15 Do-___
16 Common radio fare
17 Former New York City chief
19 Indignation
20 Banks and others
21 Kind of engineering
23 Partygoer's purchase
26 Air travel needs, for short
27 Mysterious creature
28 No-holds-barred
30 "You Gotta Start Off Each Day With a Song" singer
33 Some burger toppings
34 Do business
36 Idaho, the ___ State
37 Outlines in detail
38 Its common extensions are the theme of this puzzle
39 "The Alienist" author Carr
41 Suffix with labyrinth
42 Go (over)
43 Long-billed game bird
44 Fire starters
47 Absolution seeker
48 Aristophanes work
49 Grunted laugh
51 Loses immediacy
52 1945 Physics Nobelist Wolfgang
54 "Ecstasy" actress, 1933
56 Spring collector: Abbr.
57 Heroine who declares "I have always depended on the kindness of strangers"
62 Descendant of Aaron
63 Stick fast (in)
64 Take it easy
65 Elmer, to Bugs
66 "Family Ties" mom
67 Documentarian Morris

DOWN

1 Huck's pal
2 "Surfin' ___"
3 Actress Susan
4 Longtime N.C.A.A. basketball powerhouse
5 Mideast ruler
6 Not flimsy
7 Has a bit of
8 One of the Argonauts
9 Famous diarist
10 ___ counter
11 Like Poe's tales
12 Actress Petty
13 Grp. founded in Baghdad, 1960
18 Apparatus
22 J.F.K. posting
23 Like quaint streets, perhaps
24 "Fighting" N.C.A.A. team
25 Gypsy dance accompaniment
27 Broadway's Brynner
29 Vessel name starter
30 Area between hills
31 Fire site
32 Fire remains
34 Pairings
35 Bobble a fly, say
39 Show with many spinoffs
40 University of Michigan home
42 Butt in
45 ___ Rio, Tex.
46 Like some garnishes
47 Mideast ruler
49 Puts up
50 Quizmaster
52 Variegated
53 Singer Guthrie
54 ___ Day, March 25
55 Cut down on
58 Chat room abbr.
59 Bladed pole
60 Uniform: Prefix
61 Cardinal's home: Abbr.

by Dan Reichert

18

ACROSS

1 Terrif
4 "Ain't Too Proud
 ___"
9 Saunter
14 Education, initially?
15 Amtrak offering
16 Like some panels
 or flares
17 Emissions
 inspector's concern
19 Southern sound
20 Messenger ___
21 "Remington ___"
 of 1980s TV
23 Union agreement
24 "___ go!"
26 Dog option
28 Head of England
29 Sharp competitor
32 Lucy Lawless title
 role
33 Midway around a
 diamond
36 Betty ___
40 Wine that doesn't
 age
44 Literary governess
45 It can take the
 long or short view
46 Toast
50 Frederick's of
 Hollywood offering
51 School of
 tomorrow?
52 New York lake
 that flows into the
 Allegheny
56 Abrades
58 Place for many
 a PC
59 Limy libation
62 Degree in
 mathematics?
63 Very little, in
 recipes
65 "La Orana Maria"
 painter
68 Circus supporter
69 Wrinkly fruit
70 Wing it?
71 Pitiful
72 Treat unfairly
73 Doctor's charge

DOWN

1 Teutonic title
2 Hall-of-Fame
 football executive,
 longtime Steelers
 owner
3 Jurassic giant
4 Custom
5 "Draft Dodger
 Rag" singer
6 Doozy
7 "Someone ___
 America" (1996
 film)
8 Light, rich sponge
 cakes
9 Back at sea
10 Annihilate, with
 "down"
11 Major's successor
12 Carriage with a
 fold-down top
13 Cereal killer
18 Listen to your gut?
22 See 57-Down
24 It'll show you the
 world
25 Exxon alternative
27 Asian capital
30 Mustard, e.g.:
 Abbr.
31 Santa ___
34 Throw out
35 Gillespie, to fans
37 Cram
38 40-Across fancier
39 Lulls
41 Break down
42 Easter lead-in
43 ___ Torrijos
 Herrera, former
 head of Panama
47 Like a snob
48 Atmospheric
 pollution meas.
49 Hullabaloo
52 Seniors, e.g.
53 Couldn't help but
54 Domestic . . .
 or a title for
 this puzzle
55 What jokes are
 good for
57 With 22-Down,
 noted Taiwan-born
 film director
60 Ex-governor
 Grasso
61 Office cry
64 Camera inits.
66 Neighbor of Ger.
 and Hung.
67 Nevada county

by Frank Longo

ACROSS

1 Push hard
4 Olympic sport since 1964
8 Forgo
14 Cooler in the summer
16 Paris's Arc de Triomphe de l'___
17 Components of 38-Across
19 Flower holder
20 Sow what?
21 Pro
22 Plant with a chewable leaf
25 River in Dante's "Inferno"
27 "Got it"
30 Arab leader: Var.
32 Oil field?
34 North Sea tributary
35 Pearl Buck heroine
36 Actress/host Tyler
38 Piano exercise for beginners
42 1930s V.P. John ___ Garner
43 Travel
44 Make it
45 Use a shuttle
46 Butter up?
48 Goals of some candidates, for short
49 Wheel of a spur
51 Christiania, now
53 ___ chi
55 Take
57 Band together
61 Possible title for this puzzle
65 When many shops open
66 Regressed
67 Talked like Vito Corleone
68 Ones who are all broken up
69 Ave. intersectors

DOWN

1 Optician's display
2 ___ above
3 Arizona spring training site
4 Tabloid nickname
5 Acting legend Hagen
6 One of the original 13: Abbr.
7 About
8 Snowball thrower
9 "It's about time!"
10 Have a bawl
11 Paul Revere, for one
12 Title beekeeper in a 1997 film
13 Little brother, maybe
15 Astronaut's answer
18 Home of the Peabody Museum of Natural History
23 ___ lily
24 Master with strings
26 City near the cave of Elijah
27 Codicil, e.g.
28 When this happened
29 Clergy students
31 Supports, in a way
33 Series of online posts
35 "___ Mio"
36 Comparable in years
37 Lead ___ life
39 De ___
40 Fasten on
41 Keglers' places
46 Hit on the head
47 Chug follower
48 Aquaculturists' locales
50 Kvetch
52 Blockheads
53 Peter, for one
54 Recorded events
56 Garage job
58 Types with fat recording contracts
59 Blockhead
60 They may be split
62 Collagen target
63 Opposite of bellum
64 Whiz

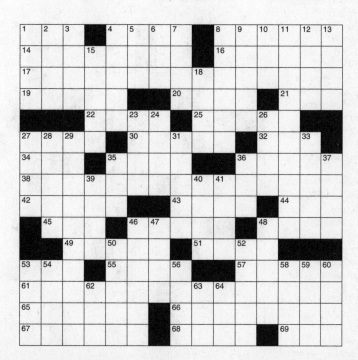

by David J. Kahn

20

ACROSS

1 Any one of a trio of Hollywood sisters
6 Reason to get some cosmetic dental work
10 ___-Americans (about 3.5 million people)
14 Say "amen," say
15 Gadzooks, e.g.
16 "You've Got Mail" actress
17 People's 2006 Sexiest Man Alive
19 Just
20 City southeast of 64-Across
21 Starting
22 Beverage brand
24 Mouth's locale
26 Cage for hawks
27 Subway stop: Abbr.
28 New York's ___ Mansion
30 Hen, e.g.
32 Julius Caesar portrayer, 1963
34 What a drinker may enter
38 Chevrolet model
39 Big exporter of coconut cream and coconut oil
41 Prefix with kinetic
42 O.K.'s
44 Frat Pack actor
46 Tasty
48 Smirk
49 Fertilized things
52 Wander
53 Like some checks
54 Quarter
56 City with una torre pendente
57 Particularly: Abbr.
60 R & B singer with a hit 1990s sitcom
61 Wishful things? . . . or a literal description of 16-, 17-, 32-, 44- and 60-Across

64 City along the Chisholm Trail
65 Fidel Castro's brother
66 Part of a printing press
67 Refuse
68 Starchy side dish
69 Points on a crescent moon

DOWN

1 Crazy
2 Like relics
3 Timber hewers
4 Poetic contraction
5 Robes, tiaras, etc.
6 Shade of brown
7 Game division
8 "Were ___ do it over . . ."
9 Insincere
10 Partner in an old radio comedy duo
11 Lets
12 Shoelace tip
13 Presidential candidate who said "No one can earn a million dollars honestly"
18 Some organic compounds
23 Water holder
25 Repeats
26 Construction worker
28 South side?
29 French dream
30 Like many cared-for lawns
31 Measure again, as a movie's length
33 Fervent
35 Computer technicians' positions
36 Everyone, in Essen

37 Blast constituent?
40 Historic Umbrian town
43 Palm type
45 Enormous
47 Sauté
49 Like an eyeball
50 "From the Earth to the Moon" author
51 "Encore!"
53 Volleyball stat
55 Annual May event, informally
56 Windfall
58 When repeated, a dance instructor's call
59 Most are 3, 4 or 5
62 Top bond rating
63 Bearded beast

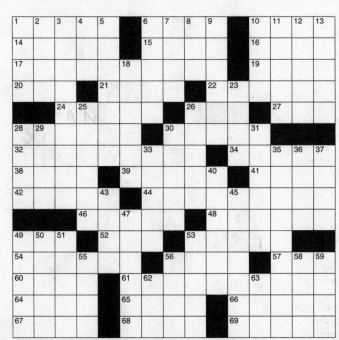

by E. J. Platt

ACROSS

1 It may wash out bridges and embankments (as in this puzzle)
6 Onetime White House scandal
10 Salt source
13 Afghan's neighbor
14 Secure
15 Scotland Yard discovery
17 Honey bunch?
18 Actress with an uncredited part in "Zoolander"
20 Bedazzles
22 Get to, in a way
23 Common ___
24 In case this is of interest . . .
25 With 49-Across, famous line from "The Rime of the Ancient Mariner"
31 Not just swallow
35 City NW of Orlando
36 Depraved
37 Item that may be "Miss" printed?
38 Ingredient in a Caribbean cocktail
39 Took a pleasure excursion
42 Visit Sundance, maybe
43 One of Charlie's Angels
45 Covered walk
46 Large vocal group
48 Cuarto de baño, e.g.
49 See 25-Across
51 Field of note?: Abbr.
53 The difference between regular mail and e-mail?
54 Batter's hope
57 Canon composer
63 Bialy, e.g.
65 "Me, too"
66 Distinguish
67 Craft that pulled over for Sirens
68 Old World relative of a canary
69 It's springless
70 Source of a stream
71 Hydrogeologist's concern

DOWN

1 Hooch
2 Hubbard of Scientology
3 Kiln
4 Like a short film
5 Chaos
6 Big inits. in car financing
7 Top-of-the-line
8 A gazillion
9 Before, in poetry
10 Panoramic photos, say
11 Pizazz
12 Rocket scientist's prefix
16 Canal, e.g.
19 "___ I?"
21 Hillbilly's negative
24 Sovereign
25 Tears, metaphorically
26 TSX maker
27 Sri Lankan tongue
28 "Boston Legal" broadcaster
29 Lake divided by a state line
30 Spanish 101 verb
32 Rush
33 Glacial deposit
34 Onetime White House scandal
40 "___ Death" ("Peer Gynt" piece)
41 Maine
44 When repeated, a response to "What's new?"
47 A Clinton
50 Derisive cry
52 Egyptian tomb item
54 Big trouble
55 Apartment next to a super, maybe
56 Distance between some posts
57 Look (over)
58 Tiny pond-dweller
59 Knucklehead
60 Caustic comment
61 Runner Zátopek
62 Main
64 Big cheer

by Lee Glickstein and Craig Kasper

ACROSS

1 Malicious one
6 Country music legend Ernest
10 Poverty and war
14 Related on the mother's side
15 Oil that's not really oily
16 Board unit?
17 Relative of "It's not you, it's me"
20 Co. name ender
21 Girl who's having a ball
22 Like some expensive tickets
23 Actor McGregor
25 Prepared
27 "Chasing ___," 1997 film
28 Two tablets every 12 hours, say
30 Mother of Ares
32 Cry of disgust
35 Jimmied
37 "Bye Bye Bye" boy band
39 Almost zero
43 Rule to follow
44 1979 Vanessa Redgrave title role
45 '50s political inits.
46 Kind of skirt
48 Rowers
52 The husband's
53 Old hand
55 "___ Sutra"
56 Judge
60 Yalie
62 Certain corp. takeover
63 "We have a big dessert coming"
66 Trim
67 Alternative media magazine
68 Title boy in old comics

69 They may be hard to beat
70 Tap-in, e.g.
71 Follows

DOWN

1 Hidden
2 Bisected
3 Cuddly zoo animals
4 Hot time in Québec
5 Rush, e.g.
6 Repeated part of a soliloquy
7 Einstein's birthplace
8 Dark horses
9 How many vacationers travel
10 Suggest
11 Bound
12 Some frills
13 Source of many spills
18 Leave
19 Fox with the 1988 hit "Naughty Girls (Need Love Too)"
24 Borderline agreement?
26 Classic name in retail clothing . . . or a hint to this puzzle's theme
29 Blanch
31 Dame ___
32 Memo starter
33 B & B
34 Ticker tape, for short?
36 Shade of black
38 Predator
39 Rockets can be found in this: Abbr.

40 Check out
41 Some T-shirts
42 He played Lord Jim in "Lord Jim"
47 Deplete
49 1992 and '96 Dream Team member
50 Represent
51 Campbell and Judd
52 Allergic reaction
54 Convened again
56 Meat dish often served with gravy
57 Go through
58 Good college for poets?
59 VW predecessor
61 Words of affirmation
64 It touches four Great Lakes: Abbr.
65 Deprive (of)

by Pete Muller

ACROSS

1 Shark rival
4 Rosemary and sage
10 National, previously
14 Flurry
15 Berate
16 Pick stuff up
17 Manipulative technique
19 Parks of Alabama
20 Letter that's not really at the end of the Greek alphabet
21 She, in Italy
22 Web surfer, e.g.
23 They can carry a tune
26 Thrown in the air
28 Discrimination against a majority
31 "Dallas" mother
33 Baloney
34 Kind of consciousness
36 Asian capital whose name means "place of the gods"
40 More lustrous
42 Lay off
44 Kicking dance
45 Over and over
47 Stand at home?
48 Booker, at times
50 What mirrors show
52 Something in the air
55 New Zealand native
57 Satisfy
58 Stage actress Caldwell and others
60 Watch part
64 Arctic exclamation
65 Search-by-definition tool

68 Film lead-in for Cop
69 Love letter salutation
70 Make it while the sun shines
71 Checkup
72 Puts forth
73 Casual greetings

DOWN

1 Rapper who co-founded Roc-a-Fella Records
2 Hipness
3 Binge
4 Hit sign
5 "That'll show him!"
6 Put through a sieve
7 Novel that begins "Stately, plump Buck Mulligan . . ."
8 Low pitch
9 Minnesota twin?
10 Red Sox fans' slogan until 2004
11 Nelson Mandela's native tongue
12 Sits for a shot
13 Eyeball benders
18 Like some church matters
24 Bundle
25 Shield border
27 Heineken, e.g.
28 Richie's mom, to the Fonz
29 Play alone
30 Coast-to-coast hwy.
32 Future atty.'s hurdle
35 Middle name of The King
37 Rhyme scheme of the "Rubáiyát"
38 Kingdom in a 1951 Broadway musical
39 No pro

41 Home equity conversion
43 "Eso ___" (Paul Anka hit)
46 N.S.A. headquarters near Baltimore
49 It may cause a breakdown
51 Knack
52 Card game without 8's, 9's and 10's
53 Copy
54 San Francisco's ___ Buena Island
56 Grant portrayer in 1970s–'80s TV
59 Endangered antelope
61 Hurting
62 "Ta-ta!"
63 "Grand" brand
66 Granola grain
67 Auditing org.

by Ben Tausig

24

ACROSS

1 In
5 Fling
10 Places to cool one's jets?: Abbr.
14 Runner's assignment
15 Requiring extra postage, say
16 River to the Colorado
17 "I am not a doctor, but I play one on TV," e.g.
19 Landing pad for Santa
20 More copious
21 Charisma
23 Kaufman or Rooney
25 Furniture woods
26 Aaron and Raymond
29 Foreign dignitaries
33 End in ___
34 Tristan's love
35 Jr.'s junior
38 This completed puzzle has 10 of them, each three letters long, reading diagonally
41 Adult beverage
42 Puts out
43 Algonquian Indian
44 Money maker
45 "Who's there?" response
46 Not achieved
49 ___-masochist
51 Relates
55 Social crusader's wish
59 ___ de vivre
60 Kids' art class staple
62 Nos. on checks
63 "Maria ___," Jimmy Dorsey #1 hit
64 Curved molding
65 Japanese soup
66 Homeys
67 Not currently in use, as a theater

DOWN

1 "The West Wing" actor
2 Cripple
3 Police dept. title
4 Professed
5 Result of a breakup?
6 Architect I. M. ___
7 Stair alternative
8 At any time
9 Jane who was courted at Thornfield Hall
10 Suits, with "with"
11 Pop singer Apple
12 Veto
13 They may be found behind paintings
18 Lorgnette part
22 Sore throat cause
24 Conditional agreement starter
26 ___ Men with the 2000 hit "Who Let the Dogs Out"
27 Govt.-regulated business
28 Tease mercilessly
30 Masquerade costume for two
31 Grayheads
32 Popular ice cream
34 Wise to
35 Some bargain bin contents: Abbr.
36 News clipping
37 "Gotcha!"
39 Pal of Patsy on "Absolutely Fabulous"
40 Tornado or earthquake
44 To a greater extent
45 13th or 15th
46 Clear, in a way
47 Ruth's mother-in-law
48 Formal orders
50 Rich tapestry
52 Angry, with "off"
53 "Enchanted" girl in a 2004 film
54 Old World duck
56 Gymnast Korbut
57 One who's sadder and maybe wiser
58 Hardly warlike
61 School subj.

by Patrick Blindauer

ACROSS
1 "No kidding!"
9 ___ mama (rum drink)
15 Enter full-force
16 One who skips church, maybe
17 Subjects of a hit 2005 documentary
19 Recess
20 Charge for using
21 Vegas V.I.P.
26 High school class, informally
27 Part of an ear
30 How 46-Across can be answered
31 Setting for a check
32 Most flamboyant
34 Con's opposite
35 Overstay one's welcome, e.g.
36 "I can't he-e-ear you . . . !"
40 Currency exchange shop abbr.
41 Architectural space above an arch
43 Thomas of "That Girl"
46 Shade of 17- and 57-Across
47 Computer storage unit, informally
48 Plenty mad
49 Coquette's trait
51 Akin
53 Double Stuf treat
57 Part of the press
62 Eventually
63 Many a door feature
64 Remove the pits from
65 This answer and others

DOWN
1 Intestinal parts
2 Sub
3 Hardly geniuses
4 Without ___ (silently)
5 Wreath material
6 Julio to julio
7 Mid.
8 #1
9 Elaine ___ of "Seinfeld"
10 Bit of scum
11 Census unit
12 Each
13 "The Freshmaker" candy
14 Some insurance frauds
18 "Or ___!"
22 "Yes, indeed!"
23 English professor's wear, stereotypically
24 Again, in music
25 When the Sup. Court's new term begins
27 TV juggernaut started 10/6/2000
28 Eponymous physicist
29 Dizzy Gillespie specialty
31 Construction site sights
33 "You don't believe me?"
34 Home, for one
37 Coat part
38 Gen. Robert E. ___
39 Math subj.
41 Not open
42 Skewer
43 Erred on
44 French rocket
45 Sends, as payment
46 Had on one's back
49 Punished with a stick
50 Second-year collegians, informally
52 Old ___, Conn.
54 Olds oldies
55 Writer ___ Stanley Gardner
56 Sweet suffixes?
58 New Deal org.
59 Instant, in slang
60 Each
61 Mil. address

by Ethan Friedman

ACROSS

1 Suffix on color names
4 Shoot upward
10 1950, in copyrights
14 DVD maker
15 In
16 Role for Ingrid
17 N.Y.C. subway inits.
18 Moves suddenly
19 Eartha Kitt role
20 Summer vacation locale
22 Peter the Great, e.g.
24 Fox's prey
25 1980 Erich Segal novel
29 A little over half the world
31 Time, in Torino
32 ___ Tomé
33 Mister
35 Deep blue
36 Dict. listing
37 Percy Sledge hit of 1966
41 Star of "The Facts of Life"
42 Where E*Trade was traded: Abbr.
43 Letter abbr.
44 Howard Hughes once controlled it
45 "Don't Bring Me Down" grp.
46 Kodak founder
50 Ang Lee film, 1994 Best Foreign Film nominee
55 Sports org. since 1906
56 Unexciting
57 Eliminates
59 Place for a Christmas card
61 Aggravation
63 It might be picked apart
64 Attack
65 City whose name is Siouan for "a good place to dig potatoes"
66 End of a four-day hol., maybe
67 Mice catchers
68 Degrades
69 Draft org.

DOWN

1 Edna O'Brien or Sinéad O'Connor
2 Shrill sound
3 John Wayne film set in Africa
4 Rubella symptom
5 Place to put the feet up
6 Office building cleaner
7 Asian peninsula
8 CPR performer
9 Go out and back in an Outback, perhaps
10 Book before Nahum
11 "___ Explains It All" (cable series)
12 Phoenix setting: Abbr.
13 Song and album by the Doors
21 Meaning
23 Like a 3-4-5 triangle
26 Verboten thing
27 One who's not in the habit of wearing a habit
28 Mafia leader
30 Some fund-raisers
34 "GoodFellas" co-star
35 Cakes' partner
37 Electric guitar attachment
38 Protect from the air, in a way
39 Singer Marilyn
40 Skims
41 Map abbr.
47 Darts
48 Mother's Day baby, e.g.
49 Dugongs' kin
51 Noodleheads
52 Drummer Gene
53 Fertilizes
54 Feminine
58 Those, to José
59 Tropical fruit
60 Wrecker's job
62 Word with sister or story

by Peter Gordon

ACROSS

1 Kind of gun
4 Catalyzing subatomic particles
9 Singe
13 Father of octuplets on "The Simpsons"
14 Picture to carry around?
16 Knock over
17 Clowns' wear
18 Pipe fitting
19 O.T. book
20 It has many pages
21 Skull and Bones member, e.g.
22 Receivers of manumission
25 Dobbin's "right"
26 Cape ___, Portugal (continental Europe's westernmost point)
28 Pocket filler
30 Link
31 Flashlight backup
36 Title for this puzzle
40 Brunch option
41 About
44 "___ I Can Make It on My Own" (Tammy Wynette #1 hit)
45 Grade schooler's reward
46 German pronoun
47 Animal that can be ridden
51 Soprano Marton
52 Not tied up, as funds
56 Ring of plumerias
57 Like Duroc hogs
58 Leader in sports
61 Put the kibosh on
62 Makeup carrier
63 Set

64 CPR deliverers
65 Wedding reception party?
66 Emerson's "___ to Beauty"

DOWN

1 Rushed headlong
2 Mission commemorated on the back of the Eisenhower dollar coin
3 Subject of annual Congressional budget debate
4 ___-Argonne offensive of W.W. I
5 Open, in a way
6 Gambling inits.
7 Highlands negative
8 Camera types, for short
9 "Shake a leg!"
10 Takes one's turn
11 Threshold for the Vienna Boys' Choir
12 Switch in the tournament schedule, maybe
14 Scans ordered by M.D.'s
15 Suffix with glass
23 Adipocyte
24 Fretted instrument
27 Words with thumb or bum
29 Car making a return trip?
30 Storage units
32 Sweet drink
33 Like staples
34 Tylenol alternative
35 Canyon area
37 Holmes to Conan Doyle, e.g.

38 Like soda crackers
39 Not choose one side or the other
41 Lead-in to a questionable opinion
42 Two bells in the forenoon watch
43 Freshly worded
48 Pool problem
49 Reagan attorney general
50 Leeds's river
53 Gremlins and others, for short
54 Little, in Leith
55 "A Wild ___" (cartoon in which Bugs Bunny first says "What's up, Doc?")
59 '60s war zone
60 U. of Md. is in it

by Byron Walden

ACROSS

1 To the extent that
8 Pebble-filled gourd
14 Sweet, dark wine
15 Inflexible
17 Spiritual leader of the Isma'ili Muslims
18 Rock band with a record-tying eight Grammys in 1999
19 Some babysitters
20 ⅛ of a fluid ounce
22 Suddenly lose it
23 Org.
24 Raft material
26 Skier McKinney
29 Marriage announcement
34 Place in which to luxuriate
37 "A ___ plan . . ."
38 1981 miniseries set in ancient Israel
39 Theater passage
41 Where bottles of alcohol sit
42 Unmitigated
43 The Crimson Tide, familiarly
44 Influence on 1980s pop
45 Clorox or Clorets
46 Melon type
48 Strong supporter?
50 Booty
54 Fancy do
58 Fastener piece
59 "The Bell Jar" author
60 Dogsled runner, maybe
62 Martin Luther King Jr.'s birthplace
64 It's drained by traveling
65 Kigali resident
66 Lower limbs
67 Trumpet blast

DOWN

1 Appliance maker
2 They may span generations
3 Portrait painter ___ Hals
4 With suspicion
5 Cheers
6 ___ fin (at last): Fr.
7 Danger for a riverboat
8 "Mississippi ___" (1992 film)
9 Portrait on an old 2¢ stamp
10 Succumbed to fear, maybe
11 Ledger entries: Abbr.
12 James of Hollywood
13 Tolstoy heroine
16 Pick
21 ___ avis
25 Double platinum Genesis album of 1981
27 Actress Plummer
28 Brewer's need
30 Cry (for)
31 Captures
32 Can. borderer
33 ___ Lee
34 Healing sign
35 One of Henry VIII's six
36 Name on a razor
38 Doll's utterance
40 Showing fatigue
41 One-fourth of a barbershop tune
43 Pastoral sounds
46 Noises from a rattletrap
47 Obliquely
49 Acknowledge
51 Fish in a John Cleese film
52 Perfume
53 Lake Volta's locale
54 Funny bit
55 "What a pity!"
56 Punishment for a pirate
57 Movie dog
59 Builder's need
61 Big 12 team: Abbr.
63 Old name in travel

by Patrick Berry

ACROSS

1 Person of letters?
7 Picker-uppers
15 Pique
16 Prairie State
17 Peanut brittle base
18 Puts faith in
19 Preceders of G
20 Pusan soldier
22 Pair of filmmaking brothers
23 Perfidious clerk in "David Copperfield"
24 Practically no time
27 Pamphlet with a "Draw Me" challenge
29 Pageantry
33 Phoenix neighbor
35 Paternity identifier
36 Personal: Prefix
37 Pretty souvenir
41 Play's ___'acte
42 "Protect mine innocence, ___ fall into the trap . . .": "King Henry VIII"
43 Portree's isle
44 Port-of-call call
45 Pay no heed to smoking rules
48 Parisian thought
49 Paulina's "other"
53 Paper towel-touting waitress
57 Pisa monk's title
58 Peter Sellers parodied him in "Murder by Death"
59 Pair on a head
62 "Princess Ida" follow-up operetta, with "The"
64 Pacific wriggler
65 PC info
66 Pulsating sound, informally
67 Potato, meat and sauce dish

DOWN

1 Pirate's eye cover
2 Partly eat away
3 "Payment not required"
4 Pepperidge Farm offering
5 Peer Gynt's mother
6 Profligately eye
7 Preserved food in jars
8 Pop grp. heard in "Xanadu"
9 Phenomena or personae: Abbr.
10 Practice economy, when preceded by 48-Down
11 Preoccupied with
12 Place last, say
13 Pride member
14 Payroll dept. ID's
21 Poetic adverb
25 ". . . perhaps comes ___ surprise . . ."
26 Penn. and others
28 President Johannes ___ of Germany, 1999–2004
29 Petty criminal
30 Performer with Krupa and Kenton
31 Peat source
32 Plant container, when preceded by 37-Down
33 Phu My Hung site, Ho Chi ___ City
34 Plasm prefix
37 Preceder of 32-Down
38 Part
39 Poetic name for Ireland
40 Pedagogical inits. in Nashville
46 Part of H.M.S.
47 Partner (with)
48 Preceder of 10-Down
50 "Push Comes to Shove" choreographer
51 Projections from a central point
52 Positive end
53 Prisoner's tool for escape
54 "Phew! Finally ___ know!"
55 P.D.Q., to a surgeon
56 Pluck or hair extension?
60 Pile
61 Pseudonym lead-in
63 Prefix with propyl

by Patrick Merrell

ACROSS

1 Cheese choice
6 It's no free ride
9 Gangster gals
14 Like a Hitchcock audience, typically
15 Grant opponent
16 Poet T. S. ___
17 Hitchhikers' needs
18 Turkish chief
19 Not completely white anymore
20 "Where did ___ wrong?"
21 Testing, as one's patience
24 S-shaped molding
25 Fear
27 Scant
29 Like 90 proof liquor
30 Non-Rx
31 Four Monopoly properties: Abbr.
34 European carrier
35 Bad winner's behavior
37 "Who's the ___?"
40 Peking or Siam suffix
41 Direction for a wagon train
42 Large turnip
45 ___ good clip
47 Valuable rock
48 Spying device
49 Reviewer
53 Outsiders may not get it
56 Put a new handle on
57 Ticklish Muppet
59 Thick-skinned critters
61 33⅓ r.p.m. spinners
62 Many a pope
64 Before, in poetry

65 California team [and 18 letters in the grid to circle . . . and then connect using three lines]
67 Lightly burn
68 N.Y.C. ave. between Park and Third
69 Red Square notable
70 Gang's slanguage
71 Allow
72 Newsboy's shout of old

DOWN

1 Comic page offerings
2 Scale reading
3 Not outside
4 Memphis-to-Mobile dir.
5 Troubadour's six-stanza verse
6 Pot composition
7 Sponsorship
8 Gardener's vine support
9 Dr.'s field
10 Stews
11 Common Valentine's Day gift
12 Theater section
13 Eye ailment
22 Lively piano pieces
23 Córdoba cat
26 ___ nova (1960s dance)
28 Zenith competitor
32 Surgical assts.
33 ___ Snorkel
35 Fed. purchasing org.
36 Wit who wrote "When in doubt, tell the truth"
37 Sis's sib

38 Your and my
39 Hot under the collar
40 Shade of white
43 U.K. radio and TV inits.
44 Violinist Leopold
45 Prefix with 25-Across
46 Railroad support
50 Skill
51 Damage
52 Business jet maker
54 Zaire, now
55 "Yes ___, Bob!"
57 She, in Roma
58 Bandit's refuge
60 Call in a bakery
63 Holiday in Vietnam
66 Bewitch

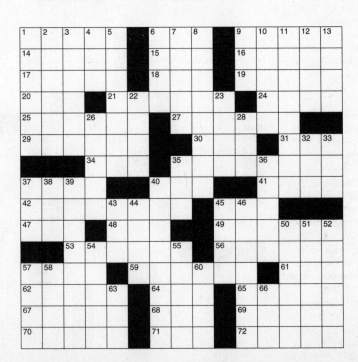

by Patrick Merrell

ACROSS

1 Hate or fear follower
5 Accra's land
10 Held up
14 Actress Skye
15 Like some beans
16 Golf club
17 Pen denizens
18 Jumped between electrodes
19 Retin-A treats it
20 Jungle crusher
22 Hostile incursion
24 Line C, maybe, in a voting booth: Abbr.
25 Bullet point
26 Quaint contraction
29 All there is
33 Fish in a John Cleese film
34 Inner: Prefix
35 It may follow a cut
36 Justice Fortas
37 Athrob
40 Badge issuer, for short
41 Kind of crime
43 Court statement
44 Phantom's haunt
46 Ready to freak out, maybe
48 Stable parents
49 Pencil-and-paper game
50 Brain scan: Abbr.
51 Response to "Gracias"
54 Brezhnev's successor
59 Scads
60 Busey and Coleman
62 Actress Conn
63 Bring under control
64 Excite
65 Maple genus
66 Caught some rays
67 Philosopher Georges
68 Miss Liberty, e.g.

DOWN

1 Santa ___
2 "Tell me more"
3 Sicilian city
4 Cancel
5 Thou
6 Source of a thundering sound
7 Chad's place
8 Family tree word
9 Ell, maybe
10 Moved like army ants
11 Bonkers
12 Mrs. Chaplin
13 Joined at the altar
21 Draft status?
23 Calif. neighbor
25 ___ rubber
26 Mop wielders
27 Something to kick
28 Lend ___ (listen)
29 Still not happy
30 Direct elsewhere
31 Buffalo skater
32 Walt Disney's middle name
34 Those girls, in Grenoble
38 Forces out of the spotlight
39 Stupid oaf
42 Gave a goolball
45 Asian shrines
47 Groundskeeper's supply
50 Bygone auto
51 Bygone auto
52 Pizazz
53 Iditarod terminus
54 1981 hit film with a 5'3" lead actor
55 Wall St. letters
56 Early Briton
57 Old music halls
58 Patience, e.g.
61 "I'll take that as ___"

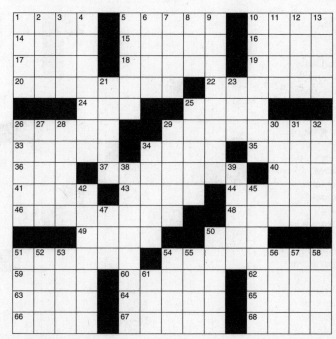

by David Pringle

ACROSS
1 Soup line
9 Erased
14 One might request help getting started
16 Inclined . . . or flat
17 Makes something up
18 Roman land
19 Company once taken over by Carl Icahn
20 "So sorry"
22 Mr., abroad
24 Southwestern sign-off
25 Reminds a bit too much
26 Like Indians
28 Suffix with jardin
29 Irish Sea feeder
30 Jazz fan, most likely
32 Rubens painted her
35 Decor finish?
37 Figs. in identity theft
38 Goes off
42 Like a lottery winner, typically
46 Boomer's kid
47 He played J-Bone in "Johnny Mnemonic"
49 Quaint schoolroom item
50 "No ___!"
52 Belle's beau
54 Carmaker since 1949
55 Layabouts
58 Opposite of always, in Augsburg
59 Round window
60 Tender shoot?

62 First name in TV talk
63 Whip snapper
64 They're perfect
65 Cross the line?

DOWN
1 Best Supporting Actor for "The Fortune Cookie," 1966
2 She served eight days in jail for public obscenity
3 Sub-Saharan scourge
4 Year for Super Bowl LXXXIV
5 Exploit
6 Where the Enola Gay plane was built
7 Start of a Beatles title
8 Olympic team?
9 Vision: Prefix
10 DuPont trademark
11 Made impossible
12 Steams up
13 Hypersaline spot
15 In places
21 Sub-Saharan scourge
23 1986 Indy 500 winner
27 ___ forces
31 "Ixnay"
33 Italian province
34 Gets back to, quickly
36 Foosball locale
38 Look into
39 Like some copies
40 Mentor's companion
41 Manager's terse order
43 It's a short walk from Copacabana
44 Celebrity-spotting eatery
45 "A diamond is forever" sloganeer
48 "Key Largo" Oscar winner
51 Fee to enter a poker game
53 Daughter of Zeus
56 Period in sch.
57 Out-of-commission cruisers
61 Feather holder?

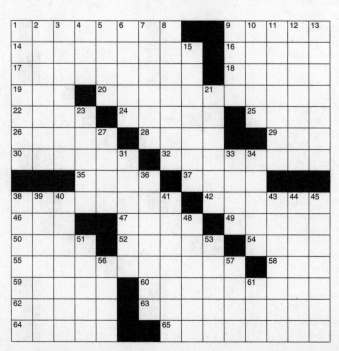

by David Quarfoot

ACROSS

1 Neighbor of Bulg.
4 Time on the job
8 Big name in morning TV
12 Joe Pesci title role
13 Silly
14 It's heard coming and going
16 ___ all-time high
17 Scary
19 Masked fighters
21 Little annoyance
22 Squeeze (out)
23 J.F.K. info
24 Word with show or know
27 Important time
28 "Too-ra-loo-ra-loo-___"
29 1952 Gene Kelly film
32 In the past
33 ___ position
34 Hall-of-Farmer Musial
35 Hoedown seats
38 Fellah
40 Going out with
41 Belgian river
42 Going nowhere fast
44 Chart-topper
45 Biblical opening
51 Snack, say
52 Title for una dama: Abbr.
53 Ancient royal
54 Grandpa Simpson
55 Despot of old
56 Othello villain
58 Novarro of "Ben-Hur"
60 Onomatopoeic Sinatra album title
64 Call at a deli
65 Senators' attire
66 "What Is to Be Done?" writer
67 No-win situations?

68 Not just tehee
69 Classic brand with an oval logo
70 UFO pilots

DOWN

1 Barker of TV/movie fame
2 Painting the town red
3 Avian talker
4 Does bad
5 Send a message in Morse code, e.g.
6 Diamond unit
7 Many a Britney Spears fan
8 Keep up
9 Subj. in which 2x+3=9 is solved
10 Stomach
11 "Not a chance, bud!"
12 Ones blowing in the wind
15 Almost eternal
18 Reid of "American Pie"
20 Has one's moment in the sun
25 Giant of note
26 "Pow!"
30 Read between the lines
31 "The Graduate" girl
34 Take effect
35 From memory
36 Turkey's place
37 Releasing one's anger
39 Cruise accommodations

40 How sweet it is!
43 It may accompany a coll. application
45 Many a news source
46 Practice, practice, practice
47 Try to knock down
48 "Anything your little heart desires!"
49 Desk sights . . . or an apt title for this puzzle
50 Lavatory label
57 Poetic tributes
59 It's put in a pot
61 Tiny battery
62 Roadside stops
63 N.F.L. Hall-of-Famer Marchetti

by Kyle Mahowald

ACROSS

1 Basic teaching
4 Sirens
9 Ruthlessly competitive
14 Start of a Tennessee Williams title
15 Red as ___
16 Spendthrift's joy
17 ___ de guerre
18 Whip on the high seas
20 Slows down
22 ___ Tech
23 Airline with the King David Lounge
24 Slander, say
26 Like "Brokeback Mountain"
30 Fix, as a pump
32 Org. with the annual Junior Olympic Games
34 Nosh
35 Hotter than hot
37 Stooge
38 Vandal
41 See 25-Down
43 Underhanded
44 Orchard Field, today
46 Buzz
48 Film pooch
49 Kind of party
50 Drug used to treat poisoning
54 Place of disgrace
56 E.T.S. offering
58 Unaccompanied
59 Spot for Spot?
60 Takes in
62 Unplanned
67 Word between two names
68 Get around
69 Military operation
70 Loaf on the job

71 Six Flags features
72 To the point
73 Some city map lines: Abbr.

DOWN

1 Lowly post
2 Something that may need boosting
3 Inner selves, to Jung
4 Annul, as a legal order
5 Apollo 13 astronauts, e.g.
6 Organization that no U.S. president has ever belonged to
7 Designer from China
8 Stop: Abbr.
9 Guiding light
10 Some fed. govt. testing sites
11 N.L. West team, on scoreboards
12 Business card abbr.
13 Venice's ___ Palace
19 Light shade
21 Cook up
25 With 41-Across, title for this puzzle
27 Reward for waiting?
28 List ender
29 ___-eyed
31 Track down
33 Arith. process
36 Still red inside
37 Burger topper
38 Show-off

39 "Here comes trouble"
40 Org. with troops
42 Ones going home after dinner?
45 Meat dish with a filling
47 100 centavos
49 Jazz buff
51 Carnival treats
52 Notwithstanding
53 Mathematical groups
55 MS. enclosures
57 Slot car, e.g.
61 Old dagger
62 Serve, as a banquet
63 Year in Trajan's reign
64 Kept
65 St. Paul hrs.
66 Rush

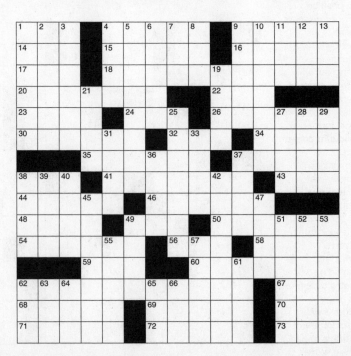

by David J. Kahn

ACROSS
1 Picnic staple
5 Lincoln and others
9 Skiing mementos?
14 Puncture
15 "The Last of the Mohicans" woman
16 Playwright Fugard
17 Actor Morales
18 Make
19 Isabel, for one
20 Condescend
22 Rodeo performer
24 Good or bad name, informally
25 Sprint
28 Advantages
31 Classic Paris couture house
32 Poured
33 Haiti, once
37 Kind of orch.
38 Friend, slangily
39 Oxford letters
40 Without a regular schedule
44 Spanish entree
47 Concert wind
48 Having I-strain?
49 President
53 One of a pair of conjunctions
54 Novelist Gide
55 As yet
59 Sci-fi figure
61 "Tobermory" writer
63 Singular, to Caesar
64 "__ Mio"
65 Currier's partner
66 Uncommon trick taker
67 Goes (for)
68 __ Gwyn, mistress of Charles II
69 Neptune's realm

DOWN
1 Tool holder
2 Shake
3 Asia's Trans __ mountains
4 Prefight event
5 Crackerjack
6 Gets on
7 Kind of message
8 Los Angeles harbor site
9 Small bag
10 Got down
11 Bake in a shallow dish
12 Opposite of flabby
13 Haphazardly
21 Botticelli figure
23 Adams of "The Ernie Kovacs Show"

26 __ Brooks, 1950s–'60s "Meet the Press" host
27 Not go straight
28 __ Major
29 Week or month at the office, usually
30 __ Valley, Calif.
33 Zap
34 Prefix with pad
35 Wearers of eagle insignia
36 Word repeated in a Beatles refrain
38 Isn't conspicuous
41 Iowa college
42 Rubs
43 Pork __
44 Canadian prov.

45 Subjects of Guinness records?
46 Struggles
48 Mideast money
49 Members of a raiding party
50 Origin of the word "troll"
51 Show eager anticipation
52 Hunger for
56 Commuting cost
57 Realm
58 Skates
60 In a bad way
62 Cuba, e.g.: Abbr.

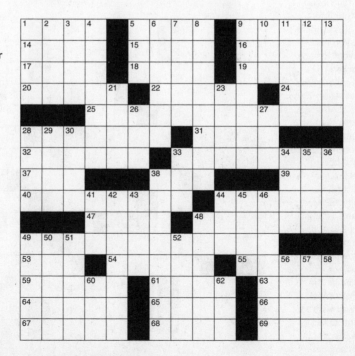

by Alan Olschwang

ACROSS

1 Pentathlon need
5 Seasonal air
10 New England team, to fans
14 Mystery author Paretsky
15 Amtrak speedster
16 Speckled steed
17 Top line
19 Eclectic mix
20 Sam and Tom, e.g.
21 Yield to gravity
23 Fruity-smelling compound
24 Center line
28 Planter's place
30 Follows closely
31 Cacophonies
34 Operatic slave
37 Addled
38 Genetic letters
39 Bottom line
41 Small songbird
42 Viewpoint
44 Biblical fall site
45 Workers' ID's
46 Timbuktu's river
47 New Ager John
49 See 62-Across
53 It may start as a grain of sand
57 "Steady __ goes"
58 "Oklahoma!" vehicle
59 Artist Miró
62 With 49-Across, where 17-, 24- and 39-Across are seen
64 It flows through Florence
65 Dean Martin song subject
66 Manicurist's tool
67 Small songbird
68 Bow over?
69 Come clean, with "up"

DOWN

1 Suffix with Kafka
2 One row on a chessboard
3 How we stand
4 Like harp seals
5 Low islands
6 Prefix with pressure
7 Actress Tara and others
8 Psalm starter
9 __ luxury
10 Isaiah or Elijah
11 Popular I.S.P.
12 Mai __
13 __-Globe
18 Actress Polo
22 Old Irish alphabet
24 Mad Hatter's guest
25 Isn't serious
26 Last name in fashion
27 Exams for aspiring D.A.'s
29 Far from firm
31 Guzzled
32 Belly button type
33 Shrewish
35 Netflix mailing
36 Is an accomplice to
39 W.W. II Japanese fighter planes
40 New Orleans-to-Detroit dir.
43 Locale for Hezbollah
45 Nottingham villain
48 Urge (on)
50 "I'm gonna make you __"
51 It's hard to do with "orange"
52 Redcap's workplace
54 An ex of Ava
55 Line holders
56 Ancient strings
58 __' Pea
59 Shoot the breeze
60 Bruins legend
61 Hydrocarbon suffix
63 "__ tu che macchiavi quell'anima"

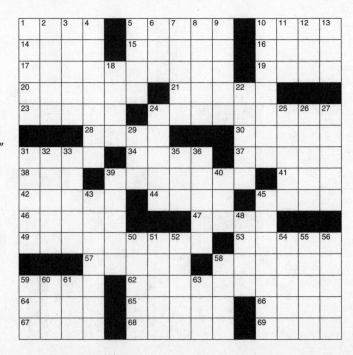

by David Kwong

ACROSS

1 Malodorous part of the farm
7 Palm Pilot, e.g.
10 Going __
14 Hockey score before overtime, perhaps
15 Three-point line's shape
16 Cartoon fish
17 Sears showroom display
18 Meatless day during W.W. II: Abbr.
19 Grizzlies or Bears
20 Apartment window sign
21 Apartment ad abbreviation
22 "Devil Inside" group, 1988
23 Barehanded
24 Icy coating
25 Grade sch. class
26 Zest
27 San Simeon castle builder
29 Hand (out)
32 "The Plague" setting
34 Bargain hunter's destination
36 Best in the polls
39 Reddish purple
40 For one
41 Actress Sommer
42 Like gymgoers
43 Bridge supports
46 Minotaur, e.g.
50 Release
52 Staff
53 Must
54 Noted race loser
56 Title girl in a song by 35-Down
57 Patio furniture material
58 "The Good Earth" heroine
59 Fell for a joke

60 Attraction
61 Tempo
62 Language suffix
63 Hang in the balance
64 Peeves
65 "__ loves you, yeah, yeah, yeah . . ."
66 Value

DOWN

1 Display a notice publicly, informally
2 Chant
3 One-quarter of 35-Down
4 Lyric by 35-Down
5 How a box may be set
6 Put out a feeler, maybe

7 Fatherland, to Flavius
8 Ringo, e.g.
9 Tip-top
10 Shenanigan
11 35-Down, once
12 Big screen
13 Thumb and others
24 Philosopher Descartes
25 In a tight spot
27 "I do __ proud man . . .": "Troilus and Cressida"
28 Things that may be saved
30 Hawaiian souvenir
31 Fraternity letter
33 Johnny __, "Key Largo" gangster
35 Focus of this puzzle

36 Buffoon
37 News org.
38 "Hey Jude" or "Help!"
39 Insert coins in, as a parking meter
44 Like the invasion led by 35-Down
45 Detest
47 Sharp
48 Gawks
49 Copier supplies
51 They help make you you
53 Nathan and others
54 Southwestern tribe
55 Banned apple spray
56 Slugger's stat.
57 Pro __

by Peter A. Collins

ACROSS

1 Iowa town where John Wayne was born
5 Zodiac symbol
9 Source of abundance
14 "___ shall unfold what plaited cunning hides": Shak.
15 Vibrations
16 Model
17 Footnote word
18 Flambéed beef entree
20 Profundity
22 Releases to fight
23 Ground
24 Ben Jonson wrote one to himself
26 "Casablanca" role
29 Censure
35 Mideast port
38 Hamburg's river
40 Dog-___
41 1962 #1 hit by the group hinted at in this puzzle's theme
44 Jumps (out)
45 Gift bearers
46 Settings in word processing
47 Nineveh's home
49 Carrier at J.F.K.
51 ___-cone
53 Qualifying races
57 Mideast capital
62 Denial
65 Carnegie Hall's main auditorium is named after him
67 "___Cop"
68 Dig
69 Music of India
70 ___ unto himself
71 1965 Beach Boys album
72 Often
73 Unexpected difficulty

DOWN

1 December festival
2 Part that's most listened to
3 OPEC V.I.P.
4 With allure
5 Lawyer's assignment
6 Dead-end jobs
7 Response to "Am not!"
8 It's heard in a herd
9 Off the mark
10 Polish prose
11 Rural expanses
12 Turner of "By Love Possessed"
13 Small water source
19 "Ad Parnassum" artist, 1932
21 Flyers' org.
25 Excavating machine
27 Sun. delivery
28 Rock's ___ Brothers
30 White House souvenir
31 One in need of a good inspection
32 Deep-sea killer
33 Trick or treat, e.g.
34 Popular ice cream
35 Pop music acronym
36 "Buenos ___"
37 Auspices: Var.
39 Jamboree grp.
42 Land on the Medit. Sea
43 Try to loosen
48 Followers: Suffix
50 "I get it!"
52 Patrick of "The Way We Were"
54 Garlicky mayonnaise
55 Go ___ for
56 Skier's wish
57 Early August
58 Not new
59 Spanish hotel reservation
60 South American rodent
61 Super-duper
63 Thus
64 Black fly, e.g.
66 Singsong syllable

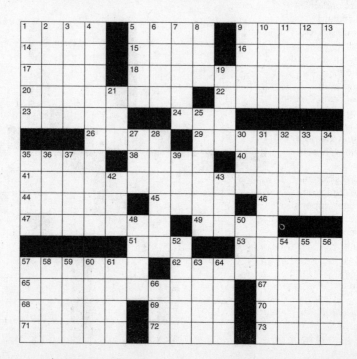

by Barry C. Silk

ACROSS

1 Makes an unexpected move
5 Captain's hires
9 Where you live
14 ___ instant
15 Dragon slayer
16 WASP part
17 See circles
20 It hangs by the neck
21 "Yep, that's the way it is"
22 Voiced admiration
23 Bottom
25 Part of NASA: Abbr.
26 Two-part
27 Did laps?
28 What a leader may give
30 Something that may be delayed by a storm: Abbr.
31 Happy guy in a musical
33 These: Sp.
34 See circles
36 Atmospheric mix
39 Cancel
40 Boxer's mitt
43 Slow on the uptake
45 Trike rider
46 10th, in a way: Abbr.
47 Bleacher feature
48 Not home
50 Homeland to Hadrian
51 Grand finale?
53 "Oh, right"
54 See circles
57 "The Emmys" author Thomas
58 Brouhaha
59 Mower maker
60 Short and maybe not sweet
61 Mary who married a future president
62 "I'm working ___!"

DOWN

1 12345, e.g.
2 Pet's choice
3 Knight in shining armor
4 Whine
5 Marker
6 Boom box button
7 Chapter in history
8 Devours, with "down"
9 Out of port
10 Some Indonesian islanders
11 Rust-causing agent
12 Half a playground argument
13 Wraps around
18 Wee bit
19 Cy Young winner Saberhagen
23 Model material
24 Home of Home Depot
27 Tend to hems
29 "A place where you have nothing to do but amuse yourself": Shaw
31 Own (up)
32 Needle
34 Hang-up
35 Destroy the interior of
36 Deteriorate
37 Eisenhower Center site
38 One at the helm
40 Helping
41 Kind of reasoning
42 Stand for bric-a-brac
44 Take home
46 Taken care of
49 One of the Earp brothers
50 ___ Friday's
52 Make a gondola go
53 Song holder
55 Bathroom, in Bath
56 Anomalous

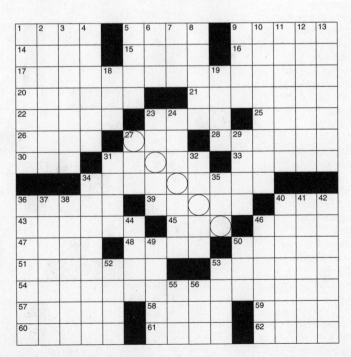

by Manny Nosowsky

40

ACROSS
1 Bow and arrow user
5 Alley cat
10 Locate
14 Trim
15 Brownish gray
16 Student's challenge
17 Reflexologists touch them
19 Missing the boat, say
20 Music instructor's cry
21 Says so
23 Getting tiresome
25 "The Canterbury Tales" character
27 Ace?
31 "Yikes!"
32 Lead-in to much
33 Crow, e.g.
38 Expense report attachment
40 "May I sew you to another sheet?" speaker
42 Tournament favorites
43 Fishing partner of 62-Down
45 Plains Indian
46 Craft store offerings
49 Road tests?
53 Supped
54 Typos
55 Football Hall-of-Famer Graham and others
59 Does runs
60 Driving exam challenge
65 One of the Sinatras
66 Black
67 "Born Free" lioness
68 Free throw value
69 Duck
70 Unappetizing serving

DOWN
1 Engagement calendar entry: Abbr.
2 Nag, maybe
3 City next to the Uinta National Forest
4 Answered
5 Name that's an alphabetic trio
6 Blacken
7 Paris's ___ de Vaugirard
8 Name
9 Cadet's reply
10 Frigid
11 Steamed
12 Archibald and Thurmond
13 Inane
18 Stag
22 Scout master?
24 Annoyance for an insomniac
25 School mtg. holder
26 ___ Crouse, 1946 Pulitzer winner for Drama
27 Some advice
28 Curved molding
29 Deal with
30 Menu offering
34 They get their kicks at Radio City Music Hall
35 Crucifix letters
36 Symbol of redness
37 Part of a Spanish 101 conjugation
39 "What ___ to like?"
41 S O S, basically
44 McBain and McMahon
47 Tickled pink
48 Like much travel
49 Pasta topping
50 Big name in pest control
51 Group of three
52 Argues sensibly
56 Rock's Jethro ___
57 Guesstimator's phrase
58 Breeze
61 "Deadwood" airer
62 See 43-Across
63 Liberal arts major: Abbr.
64 Watch

by Christina Houlihan Kelly

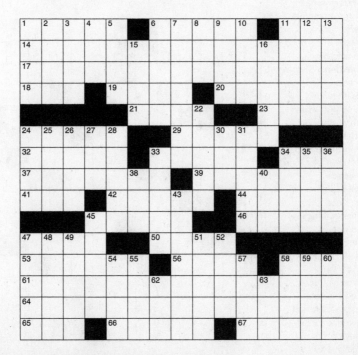

41

ACROSS

1 Greta Garbo, by birth
6 Title name after the lyric "What's it all about when you sort it out"
11 Title for a guru
14 Colorful opening course
17 Colorful spread
18 Sparkler
19 "The Dukes of Hazzard" deputy
20 Big spender, maybe
21 Journey
23 Those, to Teodoro
24 Circulating
29 Carnival sights
32 Neighbor of Ivory Coast
33 "A Mighty Fortress ___ God" (hymn)
34 French intimate
37 & 39 Colorful dessert
41 Pointed tool
42 Oscar-nominated Icelandic singer
44 Way down
45 Moon of Saturn
46 Wood carving
47 Sock style
50 Bit of Madison Ave. planning
53 Beat at a hot dog contest
56 Gay Nineties and Roaring Twenties
58 Foofaraw
61 Colorful breakfast
64 Colorful entree
65 Beverage suffix
66 Place for a swirl
67 www.yahoo.com and others

DOWN

1 Possible cause of heavy breathing
2 Finish line, maybe
3 Means of assessment
4 Place to display trophies
5 Just beat
6 Protection provider
7 Not owners
8 ___-de-lance
9 The Beatles' "___ Life"
10 "___ Wood would saw wood . . ." (part of a classic tongue twister)
11 "Snap out of it!"
12 Part of a beach kit
13 What philosophes get
15 Lady's partner
16 Suisse peaks
22 Mall station
24 Taj Mahal's home
25 "Major Barbara" playwright
26 Detective, at times
27 Resting place
28 Harry Kemelman sleuth David Small, e.g.
30 "Well, obviously!"
31 Pitch
33 Obstreperous child's cry
34 Go up against
35 Deal (out)
36 Twosome
38 Spanish eye
40 Fraternity character
43 Game on an 8×8 board
45 Nerd
47 U.S. attack helicopter
48 Like some notepaper
49 Chopin piece
51 Indo-___
52 Curse
54 Not up
55 Wrest
57 Beer, slangily
58 Throw___
59 Gambling aids
60 Kind of place
62 Biochemistry abbr.
63 Busy airport time: Abbr.

by Joseph Crowley

ACROSS

1 Old afternoon TV staple, with "The"
6 Something light and soft?
14 Misrepresented
16 Prescription description part
17 Apprehensive
18 Joining-of-hands period
19 Number of the 2016 Olympics
20 Abbr. often before a name
22 Start of a critical call
23 Get worse
24 One of two extremes: Abbr.
25 Remains on the shoulder?
29 Retreat
33 Sore loser's cry
35 "Another Green World" composer
36 Island chains
37 It's held in an orbit
38 Inventor of a braking system for cars
39 The Rhineland Campaign was part of it: Abbr.
40 Tries to outfox
44 Curiously spelled 1960 Al Cohn tune
46 Somehow
47 One locked in a boat
48 Running things in a bar
49 Slime
51 "Now I get it"
52 Rake
56 Successful result in a DNA lab
58 Certain Ontarian
60 Four-time Emmy winner for "Nick News"
61 Drunken
62 Charges
63 Something struck from a book

DOWN

1 Big maker of small cars
2 Demographic group, briefly
3 Hoops Hall-of-Famer English
4 18-Across in France
5 Head shot?: Abbr.
6 Classic caution to a child
7 Start ___
8 Prefix with tourism
9 Where singles start out in love?
10 Lustrous
11 Mythical dweller across the Rainbow Bridge
12 Broad
13 Always, in verse
15 Try to profit from
21 Tiny waves
23 Calypso relative
24 Gooper's wife in "Cat on a Hot Tin Roof"
25 "The Old Swimmin'-Hole" poet
26 Poem title start
27 Half-serious run?
28 Old Eur. money
30 Accepted
31 Hand and foot
32 "Munich" actor Ivgy
34 Spanish royalty
38 Have to return
40 Union organizers?
41 Always, in verse
42 They carry stigmas
43 Many men are registered with it: Abbr.
45 Having no charge
49 Molecular biology lab preparations
50 Some addresses
51 Unerringly, after "to"
52 Low in education
53 Frequent flier?
54 What comes to mind
55 Org. whose success is no accident?
56 Fabaceae family member
57 Breakers' equipment
59 Hardly a worthy competitor

by Michael Shteyman

ACROSS

1 Coach Bill who won three Super Bowls
6 Expert
11 Purchaser of the Victor Talking Machine Co., 1929
14 Subject of Filippino Lippi's "Allegory of Music"
15 Winter coat feature
16 Shapiro of NPR
17 "Murder in the Cathedral" playwright
18 Interval between stimulation and response
20 "Stay out!"
22 Gist
23 Wine-making city of California
24 Sets (on)
25 Savings account
28 George who co-founded the N.F.L.
32 Cured salmon
33 Madame ___, 1950s–'60s Vietnamese figure
34 Ingredient in ceramics
35 Saw about caution
39 "Hold on . . ."
40 Abbr. on some sheet music
41 ___ Moulins, Québec
42 Lively dance in duple meter
43 Sissies
46 Medical suffix
49 ___ Ski Valley
50 Study of the evolution of the universe
53 Sophomore

57 Einstein's workplace, once
59 Like biremes
60 From ___ Z
61 Certain sorority women
62 Parry
63 Ukr., once, e.g.
64 Proceeded through a traffic jam, e.g.
65 Astound

DOWN

1 Thistle, e.g.
2 Janis's partner in the comics
3 Been in bed
4 Milkmaids' aids
5 Cape Province native of old
6 Fine
7 Calendario unit

8 International arrangements
9 Michael Jackson once pitched it
10 Quite stylish, in a European way
11 Pour
12 Nile critter
13 Staffer
19 One might buy a bargain for this
21 Perfect
25 Italian grandfather
26 Shine
27 German greeting
29 Stocking material
30 Certain medical symptoms
31 Reveals
32 Bow part
34 Old deprecatory term of address

36 Wearer of kamik boots
37 Serene
38 Part of a driver's license procedure
44 Discontinue a connection
45 David, "the sweet psalmist of ___"
47 Supports
48 Strike
50 Ones working with books
51 Wild ___
52 Loud speaker
54 River of Tuscany
55 Like N.Y.C.'s Rockefeller Center
56 Linda of "Jekyll & Hyde"
58 Topper

by Dave Tuller

44

ACROSS
1 Old ___ tale
6 Fiction's opposite
10 Two-wheeler
14 Novelist Zola
15 "Are you ___ out?"
16 Luau instruments, informally
17 Wee
18 Cost of an old phone call
19 Check for a landlord
20 Game equipment for an old sitcom star?
23 Son of Seth
24 Organic salt
25 Greek T
28 ___ Kippur
29 Chem. or biol.
30 Captains of industry
32 Sudden outpouring
34 Mark in "piñata"
35 Game location for an actress?
38 Major mix-up
40 Deflect, as comments
41 IBM/Apple product starting in the early '90s
44 Pull tab site
45 Pinup's leg
48 Product pitches
49 Carved, as an image
51 Florence's river
52 Game site for a popular singer?
54 Plastic building block
57 Mélange
58 When repeated, classic song with the lyric "Me gotta go"
59 Rainbow goddess
60 Pasta sauce first sold in 1937
61 Ponders
62 Like some Steve Martin humor
63 "___ It Romantic?"
64 "Give it ___!" ("Quit harping!")

DOWN
1 Actor Snipes of "Blade"
2 Prefix with suppressive
3 Owner of MTV and BET
4 New York Harbor's ___ Island
5 Order in a bear market
6 Faithfulness
7 Licoricelike flavor
8 Hand-to-hand fighting
9 8-Down ender
10 Singer Ives
11 "I like ___" (old campaign slogan)
12 Barbie's doll partner
13 Inexact fig.
21 Train that makes all stops
22 Speaker's spot
25 Spilled the beans
26 &
27 "It's no ___!" (cry of despair)
29 Go all out
31 Like a mechanic's hands
32 Ump's call with outstretched arms
33 Paranormal ability
35 Tools with teeth
36 Wasn't turned inward
37 Tehran native
38 Place for a mud bath
39 Doze (off)
42 A ___ (kind of reasoning)
43 Maria of the Met
45 Bellyache
46 "___ Song" (John Denver #1 hit)
47 Not given to self-promotion
50 Winston Churchill flashed it
51 Love of one's life
52 Inquisitive
53 ___ mater
54 Gossipy Smith
55 Pitcher's stat
56 Beefeater product

by Elizabeth A. Long

ACROSS

1 Example of 41-Across
7 Example of 41-Across
15 Like "Survivor" groups
16 "That's fine"
17 ___ Quimby of children's books
18 Most finicky
19 Not fighting
21 Squeezed (out)
22 Ballerina's digit
23 Suffix with racket or rocket
25 Weakens, as support
29 Line up
32 Push (for)
36 Needle part
37 Mauna ___
39 Example of 41-Across
41 Theme of this puzzle
45 Example of 41-Across
46 90° pipe joint
47 Result of getting worked up
48 Call the whole thing off
50 On the wagon
54 Eton students, e.g.
56 Symbol of sturdiness
58 City map abbr.
59 Tacks on
63 Works of Swift and Wilde
66 They're over the hill
70 Dancing locale
71 "Be delighted"
72 Low tie
73 Example of 41-Across
74 Example of 41-Across

DOWN

1 Rock bands?
2 Keynote speaker, e.g.
3 Less firm
4 Instrument with a conical bore
5 Sha follower
6 French ice cream
7 Bush league?: Abbr.
8 Merle Haggard, self-descriptively
9 Sail a zigzag course
10 Little one
11 Put up with
12 Bread for a Reuben
13 Speakers' no-nos
14 Amount left after all is said and done
20 Unagi, at a sushi restaurant
24 Actress Dawson of "Rent"
26 Polar denizen
27 Polar explorer
28 Salty septet
30 Therapeutic plant
31 "___ got mail"
33 Humanities degs.
34 Memory unit
35 Cries from the woods
38 "I love him like ___"
40 Defendant's plea, informally
41 Not work out
42 Kirlian photography image
43 Four-footed TV character
44 Jar part
49 Thank-yous along the Thames
51 Black Russians may go on it
52 ___ Brothers
53 Fix, as a shoe
55 Buffalo hockey player
57 Barbecue offering
60 Bug juice?
61 Like Radio City Music Hall, informally
62 Hitch
64 Pint-size
65 "Mm-hmm"
66 Chart topper
67 "Do ___ do"
68 It may be tidy
69 ___-Cat

by Tibor Derencsenyi

46

ACROSS

1 With 1-Down, 1982 Richard Pryor/Jackie Gleason film
4 Half court game?
7 Part of an auto accident
13 Crude structure?
15 Tourist's aid
16 "Understood!"
17 Like a band of Amazons
18 Iran-Contra grp.
19 Draftsman's tool (and a hint to this puzzle's theme)
20 Satchel in the Hall of Fame
23 Little squirt
24 Poli ___
25 Aunt of Prince Harry
26 Dogma
28 Conclusion, in Germany
31 Levy on a 33-Across
33 Place to build
35 63-Across, in Málaga
36 Like vinegar
37 Cookout sites
39 Foundation exec.
40 Frank McCourt memoir
42 A few
43 Suffix with exist
45 Means of fortunetelling
47 ___ account (never)
48 "___ got it!"
50 King in a celebrated 1970s U.S. tour
51 Clampett player
52 Attend to the final detail
54 Crimson foe
55 Commits to, as an interest rate

56 Ferris in film
60 Intent, as a listener
61 Field of unknowns?
62 Hand-color, in a way
63 Rotation period
64 Muesli morsel

DOWN

1 See 1-Across
2 Shake a leg
3 Old N.Y.C. lines
4 Title guy in a 1980 Carly Simon hit
5 A Waugh
6 Any part of Polynésie
7 Where Mosul is
8 Waiter's armload
9 Guard's workplace
10 Iroquois and others
11 Grammar concern
12 Plays a campus prank on, informally
14 Gridiron formation
15 Dutch beer brand
19 Big load
20 1974 Medicine Nobelist George ___
21 Bayer alternative
22 Influential group
23 Singing Ritter
26 Implied
27 Go ___ (deteriorate)
29 Quints' name
30 Hardly strict with
32 Relative of a chickadee

34 Fashion a doily
38 Big name in cellular service
41 "___ Cheerleaders" (1977 film)
42 "I'm kidding!"
44 Brought forth
46 Endless 9-to-5 job, e.g.
49 Op-Ed, typically
51 Poem of lament
52 E. ___
53 What to call a king
54 Faulkner's ___ Varner
55 Iron pumper's muscle
56 No longer edible
57 Wall St. action
58 Diamond stat
59 Disloyal sort

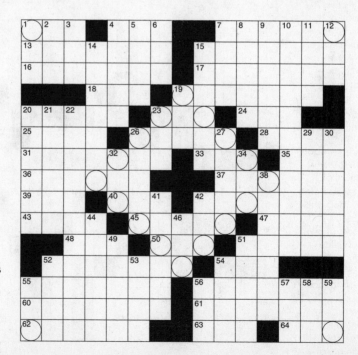

by Bonnie L. Gentry and Victor Fleming

When this puzzle has been completed, shade in the letters of 35-Across everywhere they appear in the grid, - revealing three letters and three lines.

ACROSS
1 Karate blow
5 Winkler role, with "the"
9 Cartoon pics
13 Wertmuller who directed "Seven Beauties"
14 "___ Gold"
16 Sky lights?
17 Brewery fixture
18 Knocking sound
20 Solid alcohol
22 All you need, in a Beatles song
23 Have a TV dinner, say
24 Fire sign?
26 Late singer Rawls
29 Classic Mercedes-Benz roadsters
30 Homes that may have circular drives
32 Long, long time
33 Soviet labor camp
34 Automaker Ferrari
35 July 4th message to America
40 Theological schools: Abbr.
41 Buys for brew lovers
42 Grand ___ Opry
43 How many teens go to movies
46 Not many
49 160, once
50 Mentholated cigarettes
51 Gawk (at)
53 Brief moments
54 Regains one's senses, with "up"
55 Memorable title film role of 1971
60 Some nest eggs, for short

61 Risk-taking Knievel
62 Prod
63 ___-Rooter
64 Old comics boy
65 Those, to Carlos
66 Official with a list

DOWN
1 Shutters
2 Having a gap
3 Initiations
4 "Gloria ___" (hymn start)
5 Roll up
6 Suffix with pay
7 Web
8 Fanatic
9 Adorable
10 Pond denizen
11 Mauna ___
12 Sound barrier breaker: Abbr.

15 Tend the hearth
19 Greetings of long ago
21 Early Ping-Pong score
24 Puncture
25 Enchanting
26 Horne who sang "Stormy Weather"
27 Like mud
28 3–2, en español
31 Cunning
33 Some docs
34 Masthead names, for short
35 "War is ___"
36 Green card?
37 "Phooey!"
38 Lao-___
39 "___ Fine" (1963 Chiffons hit)
40 Assn.

43 ___-doke
44 Opposite of día
45 Medicinal amount
46 Denmark's ___ Islands
47 Mistakes
48 Big name in oil
52 Snazzy Ford debut of 1955
53 Capital of Manche
54 Dict. offerings
55 Opium ___
56 Correct ending?
57 Part of a sleep cycle
58 Some football linemen: Abbr.
59 Down Under hopper

by Patrick Blindauer

ACROSS

1 King who united England
7 Game period: Abbr.
10 Hinged closer
14 Friend
15 Laramie's state: Abbr.
16 They lean to the right: Abbr.
17 Teleologist's concern
20 Word on a Mexican stop sign
21 Bugged
22 French flower
23 1/100 of a euro
24 Vainglory
25 On the side of
26 Part of the verb "to be," to Popeye
28 Overlook
32 "September 1, 1939" poet
35 Old Asian ruler
37 Jaffa's land: Abbr.
38 Figuring something out
42 A hallucinogen
43 Hanging ___ a thread
44 August 15, 1945
45 Nosedive
47 Indent setter
48 Carrier with the in-flight magazine Scanorama
49 Actress Gardner
51 Cries during a paso doble
53 "It's not TV. It's ___"
56 Make worse
60 Clunker of a car
61 Part of a city code
63 Bring to naught
64 Give the coup de grâce
65 Lamebrain, in slang
66 ___ extra cost
67 Some ESPN highlights, for short
68 Oliver Twist and others

DOWN

1 Like two dimes and four nickels
2 Without much intelligence
3 Actress Naomi of "Mulholland Dr."
4 Sony co-founder Morita
5 Post-retirement activity?
6 Bureau part
7 Places to find the letters circled in the grid
8 Use 7-Down
9 Worker who makes rounds
10 Zoo heavyweights, informally
11 On
12 MS. enclosure
13 Argued (for)
18 10th anniversary gift
19 Scandal sheet
23 Neighbor of Gabon
25 Quagmire
27 Sounds leading up to a sneeze
29 Pirate captain of legend
30 La Española, e.g.
31 Hunted animals
32 "___ Lang Syne"
33 U.S. ally in W.W. II
34 One-named singer with the 2001 hit "Thank You"
36 Exploding stars
39 Meeting expectations
40 Cagers' grp.
41 Breakfast drinks, for short
46 "Scent of a Woman" Oscar winner
48 Going out with
50 Title for one on the way to sainthood: Abbr.
52 British "Inc."
53 Artist Matisse
54 Strips for breakfast
55 Some opinion pieces
56 Old Testament book
57 Eliminate
58 Have ___ with
59 It both precedes and follows James
60 Soccer star Mia
62 Actress Long

by John Farmer

ACROSS

1 Drink garnishes
6 Seizes
11 "How about that?!"
14 Broadcast workers' org.
15 Lash of bygone westerns
16 Former
17 Antic brother
19 Fish story
20 Stitched
21 Raw resource
22 Pack, to a pack animal
24 Sticking one's nose in
27 Canine line
28 Swan's mate, in myth
29 Order in the court
33 Brigitte's friends
36 Seattle-to-Phoenix dir.
37 Sci-fi invaders
38 Title of this puzzle
43 What Alabama cheerleaders say to "gimme" four times
44 Alley __
45 "Is there no __ this?"
46 Speaks when one should stay out
49 Tidy up topside
51 Inspiring sound
52 Like many Chas Addams characters
56 Dinner table item on a string
59 '07, '08 and '09
60 Onetime E.P.A. target
62 Chinese dynasty
63 Back
66 Non-Rx
67 Absurd

68 Coffee for bedtime
69 Play for a fool
70 Wild
71 Clifford who co-wrote "Sweet Smell of Success"

DOWN

1 Takes a sharp turn
2 Violinist Zimbalist
3 Vermont ski town
4 Rolled along
5 Animal pouch
6 Praise from a choir
7 Nagano noodles
8 Heavenly altar
9 Bedroom community, briefly
10 Like some relations
11 Place to pick up valuable nuggets
12 Peace Nobelist Wiesel
13 Heaven on earth
18 Phone button
23 School basics, initially?
25 Arnaz of '50s TV
26 Big cut
30 Author Harper
31 Leave in, in proofreading
32 Petrol brand
33 Quatrain rhyme scheme
34 PC pop-up
35 Mesmerized
36 Big inits. at Indy
39 "__ certainly do not!"
40 1970s TV's "The __ Show"

41 Down-to-earth
42 Without an agenda
47 Check
48 Zhivago portrayer
49 Equine color
50 Milquetoast
53 "Laughing" scavenger
54 Pizzeria order
55 Tore into
56 10 C-notes
57 Absorbs, as a loss
58 "The Match Game" host Rayburn
61 Makes calls
64 Alternative spelling: Abbr.
65 Tokyo, once

by Courtenay Crocker and Nancy Salomon

50

ACROSS

1 Warm-blooded animal
7 Polite concurrence
14 Neighbor of Sudan
16 Behind on payments, after "in"
17 Five-pointed ocean denizen
18 Short sleeps
19 Charged particles
20 1950s Wimbledon champ Lew
21 Singer Morissette
24 Justice div. that conducts raids
25 And so on: Abbr.
28 Pepsi and RC
29 Viewer-supported TV network
30 Sag
32 E. ___ (health menace)
33 Help
34 Sportscaster Howard
35 Opposite WSW
36 Creature suggested by this puzzle's circled letters
38 ___ v. Wade
39 Criticize in a petty way
41 Cleaning tool in a bucket
42 Turner who sang "Proud Mary"
43 ___ firma
44 ___ Bartlet, president on "The West Wing"
45 Trigonometric ratios
46 Michigan's ___ Canals
47 Sn, in chemistry
48 Unpaired
49 Threadbare

51 "What were ___ thinking?"
52 Driver's levy
55 Drinkers may run them up
59 Kansas expanse
60 Back: Fr.
61 Coarse-haired burrowers
62 2001 Sean Penn film

DOWN

1 Enero or febrero
2 "You ___ here"
3 "Mamma ___!"
4 Where Moses got the Ten Commandments
5 Stella ___ (Belgian beer)
6 Tilts
7 Regatta boats

8 ___ Good Feelings
9 Spanish Mlle.
10 Darners
11 Tiny battery type
12 Dadaist Jean
13 Editor's work: Abbr.
15 ___ poetica
21 One of two in "résumé"
22 Cuckoos
23 Fast, in music
24 Body's midsection
26 Jewelry for a sandal wearer
27 Rank below brigadier general
29 Cherry seed
30 Uno y uno
31 "The magic word"
33 1 or 11, in blackjack
34 Saucer's go-with

36 Suffix with pay
37 Pea's home
40 Fade
42 "Tip-Toe Thru' the Tulips" singer
44 They cause bad luck
45 ___ Mist (7 Up competitor)
47 Characteristic
48 Puppeteer Lewis
50 Other, south of the border
51 Abbr. in TV listings
52 Tach measure, for short
53 ". . . man ___ mouse?"
54 River to the Rhine
56 D.D.E. defeated him
57 Playtex item
58 Half a year of coll.

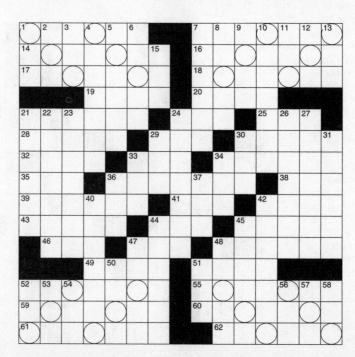

by Peter A. Collins

ACROSS

1 "Get out of here!"
5 Scott who draws "Dilbert"
10 Heart problem
14 Tortoise's race opponent
15 Argue against
16 Attempt at a basket
17 Fe, chemically
18 Actress Verdugo
19 Loving strokes
20 Course option
23 Hold the wheel
24 "___ So Fine," #1 Chiffons hit
25 Double curve
28 Old photo shade
32 Space cut by a scythe
34 ___ Khan
37 Response option
40 Ballet skirt
42 Dweller along the Volga
43 Signal hello or goodbye
44 Electric light option
47 Hedge plant
48 Person under 21
49 Group singing "Hallelujah!"
51 Sault ___ Marie
52 Stout drink
55 Parts to play
59 Quiz option
64 Advertising award
66 "Praise be to ___"
67 Lhasa ___
68 Easter servings
69 String bean's opposite
70 Person under 20
71 Optometrists' concerns
72 Department of ___
73 Ocean eagle

DOWN

1 Freighters, e.g.
2 Diamond weight
3 Came up
4 Tightens, with "up"
5 Space
6 Place to get an egg salad sandwich
7 Eve's second son
8 Chew (on)
9 Old hat
10 Nile nippers
11 Shoo off
12 Mouth-burning
13 Travelers from another galaxy, for short
21 Glenn of the Eagles
22 Professional grp.
26 Comedian Martin
27 "The Taming of the ___"
29 Consumers of Purina and Iams food
30 Vidi in "Veni, vidi, vici"
31 Playful trick
33 Opposite ENE
34 They're smashed in a smasher
35 "Go fast!," to a driver
36 Back then
38 Courtroom affirmation
39 Western U.S. gas giant
41 Carrier of 13-Down
45 Berlin Mrs.
46 Take on, as employees
50 Spin
53 Pages (through)
54 Key of Mozart's Symphony No. 39
56 Outcast
57 Ruhr Valley city
58 Gem
60 One of TV's "Friends"
61 ___Vista (search engine)
62 Final
63 Mule or clog
64 Revolutionary Guevara
65 Make, as a wager

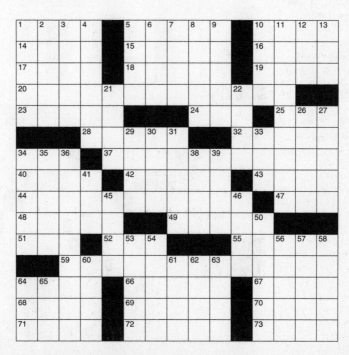

by Kurt Mengel and Jan-Michele Gianette

ACROSS

1 Bank security devices
5 Go postal
9 Betray, in a way
14 Grp. with crude interests?
15 Zip
16 Daughter of Juan Carlos I
17 Yukon, e.g.: Abbr.
18 ___ epic scale
19 Symbol of neutrality
20 Chapeau holder, spelled out in detail?
23 With hands on hips
24 Egypt and Syria, once: Abbr.
25 Targets of some beatings, spelled out in detail?
32 Part of A.C.C.: Abbr.
35 Singer Lennon
36 Begin
37 Latched
39 Unbolt, poetically
41 & 42 Somewhat
45 Union joiner of 1896
48 Bad thing to break
49 1930s–'40s tyrant, spelled out in detail?
52 European skyline sight
53 Certain electron tube
57 Illusions, spelled out in detail?
62 Oily
63 Honey, in Le Havre
64 Souvenirs with scents

65 From here
66 Men's store section
67 Pari-mutuel
68 Like some kitchens
69 Epilogs
70 Black as night

DOWN

1 Terra ___
2 Take ___ (glance)
3 Cousin of danke
4 Save's partner
5 Carnival treat
6 Half of Mork's sign-off
7 Man who was never born
8 Amount to fry
9 One may use hand signals
10 Judd's role on "Taxi"

11 Thing to have a stake in
12 Grimm beginning
13 Scottish turndown
21 Diamond stats
22 Cub scouts
26 Universal ideal
27 Suggestions
28 Bank alternative
29 Plane or square, e.g.
30 Mystique
31 Slow-cook
32 Starting
33 By way of, briefly
34 Dilly
38 Pro ___
40 Numerical suffix
43 Let up
44 Successful pitch

46 Ingenuous
47 Bickerer in the "Iliad"
50 Most recent news
51 Marketplace
54 Cineplex ___ (old theater chain)
55 Mars or Mercury
56 Southend-on-Sea site
57 Typhus carrier
58 Isn't informal?
59 Year in Diocletian's reign
60 Declaration of participation
61 Wasn't honest
62 Cow or sow

by Bruce F. Adams

ACROSS

1 Emphatic agreement
5 Pitcher Shawn ___
10 See 48-Down
14 Circular announcement
15 Ring
16 Mine, in Montréal
17 X
20 Unusual
21 Pulls down, so to speak
22 Méditerranée, par exemple
23 You may flirt with it
26 Thun's river
27 "Farewell, My Lovely" novelist
31 Neighbor of an Afghani
34 Bohr's study
35 ___ y plata (Montana's motto)
36 X
40 Hollywood job: Abbr.
41 It means nothing to Nicolette
42 "Shake, Rattle and Roll" singer
43 Sticky situation
46 Crop
47 Sorry soul
49 Authority on diamonds?
52 "I don't buy it"
55 7,926 miles, for the earth
57 X
60 ___-eyed
61 Judging group
62 Fall preceder, perhaps
63 Throw out
64 Like God, in a fire-and-brimstone sermon
65 Some queens

DOWN

1 Land bordering Bhutan
2 Equivocal answer
3 Dramatist Rice
4 North Platte locale: Abbr.
5 No dessert for a dieter
6 Climbs, in a way
7 X X X
8 Source of lean red meat
9 Clinton, e.g.: Abbr.
10 Baseless rumor
11 Archer of myth
12 Square setting
13 Faults
18 Make a father
19 Neato
24 Less woolly, perhaps
25 Author Janowitz
26 Singer DiFranco
28 Hang out
29 Noted Folies Bergère designer
30 Like some outlooks
31 Operation Desert Storm target
32 Unilever brand
33 Girl lead-in
34 Conflagrant
37 What cleats increase
38 Greg's sitcom wife
39 Labor org. since 1935
44 They may be sour
45 Whimper
46 How brutes behave
48 With 10-Across, ocelot and margay
49 Complete change of mind
50 Excellence
51 Gets ready
52 "Over here!"
53 Minuteman's place
54 They have participating M.D.'s
56 James of jazz
58 Grp. monitoring emissions
59 ___ Clemente

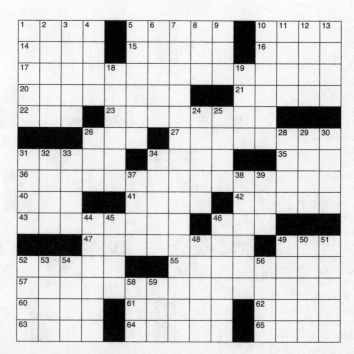

by William I. Johnston

54

ACROSS

1 New York stadium name
5 Classic toothpaste
10 Vacation spot
14 Fish for
15 Chopper blade
16 Loathsome one
17 With 27- and 47-Across, a philosophy prof's remark
20 Part of many addresses
21 Brenner Pass's region
22 Try to open a jar, say
23 Old Mideast union: Abbr.
25 With 56-Across, three-time Masters winner
27 See 17-Across
36 "___ I known!"
37 Restrain
38 Knot
39 "Where Do ___?" ("Hair" piece)
40 "The Sopranos" weapon: Var.
42 Legal scholar's deg.
43 Keep an ___ the ground
45 Mötley ___
46 It comes at a premium
47 See 17-Across
51 Repeated cry to a vampire
52 Wasn't brave
53 Pvt.'s goal?
56 See 25-Across
60 Merry dos
64 Wiseacre's reply to the prof
67 Russian poet Akhmatova
68 Bursts (with)
69 Israel
70 Crayolalike
71 Like ___ (with equal probability)
72 Masculine side

DOWN

1 Stamp on an order
2 Bell-shaped lily
3 Caraway, e.g.
4 Barely make
5 Ruffle
6 Publicize
7 Suspect's demand: Abbr.
8 King Hussein's queen
9 Melodically
10 Leonard Bernstein's "___ Love"
11 Hotel freebie
12 Resting place
13 Drain sight
18 Quiz
19 Part of a contract
24 Singer McEntire
26 January holiday inits.
27 Swindler
28 Helmeted comics character
29 Love
30 Buster?
31 Eye site
32 Atwitter
33 City invaded by Tamerlane, 1398
34 "The Hobbit" character
35 ___ a high note
40 Order in a kids' card game
41 Sympathy evoker
44 Poet Hughes
48 Opera's Scotto
49 Slumps
50 Very stylish
53 Mouthful
54 Four-time Gold Glove winner Tony
55 Wildcat
57 When people take tours in Tours?
58 Gulf port
59 Major-___
61 Film princess
62 Soon
63 It has bars
65 Knack
66 "C'___ la vie!"

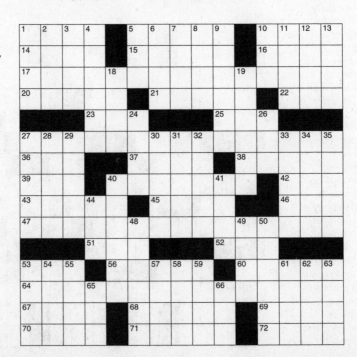

by Jim Page

ACROSS

1 Menus, essentially
6 Magnum and others: Abbr.
9 Edward Jones Dome team
13 Tee off
14 See 46-Across
15 Think out loud
17 Swedish tennis star's favorite movie?
19 Match play?
20 Capek play
21 Singer who really cuts the mustard?
23 Letters' partner
25 Works accepted as authentic
26 Madrigal accompaniment
27 Trial
29 Not sweet
31 Sábado or domingo
32 Tiny bit
34 Blew a gasket
36 Vehicle for touring Scandinavia?
40 Kind of concerto
41 Your of yore
42 "Uncle Tom's Cabin" girl
43 Time off?
46 With 14-Across, what latecomers may miss
50 Spring period
52 ___ del Sol
54 Livy's love
55 Chinese dish that casts a spell?
58 J.F.K. abbr.
59 Keep ___ out for
60 Coxcombs (and a hint to solving this puzzle)
62 Place atop
63 Prefix with annual
64 Wet spots
65 It may be ear-piercing
66 Like Nasdaq securities: Abbr.
67 Words before "Remember" and "Forget," in song titles

DOWN

1 A-mazing animal?
2 Wound
3 Sty cacophony
4 Rocky hilltop
5 Harmony, informally
6 Manner of speaking
7 Make housebound, as by bad weather
8 Hearing aides
9 Pike
10 You may get fooled when it arrives
11 Think wrongly of
12 More stuck up
16 Supreme Court, for one
18 Prolific
22 Wind dir.
24 Aid in reaching a high shelf, maybe
28 Bucolic
30 "Snow White" meanie
33 No. after a no.
35 It may have boxes and boxers
36 Change for a fin
37 "I Love Rock 'n Roll" rocker
38 Like vision in bright light
39 Italy's ___ Islands
40 "Chicago" vamp and others
44 Cologne cry
45 Approach
47 "Doesn't matter to me"
48 Reply to the impatient
49 Former Conn. governor Ella
51 "Nuts ___!"
53 Fencing, e.g.
56 Thrill
57 Cluster
61 Be discordant

by David J. Kahn

ACROSS

1 Scotland's ___ Fyne
5 It's nothing to speak of
10 Perennial presidential campaign issue
14 Memo phrase
15 Part of a U.S. census category
16 "Did you ___?!"
17 Bound
18 Manly apparel
19 ___ avis
20 Half of a decoder ring
23 Former nuclear power org.
24 "Cómo ___ usted?"
25 Maserati, e.g.
29 It gives you an out
34 The Buckeyes: Abbr.
35 Heralded
38 What a rubber produces?
39 Secret message
43 Hall-of-Fame coach Mike
44 Author Wiesel
45 Clay, after transformation
46 English essayist Sir Richard
48 Unpleasant ones
51 Landers and others
54 Opus ___
55 Other half of the decoder ring
61 Thailand, once
62 More than hot
63 Gave the go-ahead
65 French 101 verb
66 Pluralizers
67 Woman of the haus
68 Its motto is L'Étoile du Nord: Abbr.
69 Thomas Jefferson, religiously
70 Inevitability

DOWN

1 Not-so-apt word for Abner
2 Suitable for service
3 Shore catch
4 One who's beat but good?
5 "Be well"
6 Catchphrase from "Clueless"
7 Poppycock
8 They may be made with Bibles
9 Present
10 Be rough with the reins
11 Flattened figure
12 Earthwork
13 Madrid Mme.
21 Big holiday mo.
22 Notched
25 Makes origami
26 Comparatively healthy
27 Deluxe accommodations
28 All-night party
30 Early auto
31 Zhou ___
32 Move like a 3-Down
33 Tournament round
36 Nothing
37 Smile
40 Classic Jaguar
41 Hit 1980s–'90s NBC drama
42 Car safety feature
47 Coveted
49 Et ___ (footnote abbr.)
50 Warn
52 Hospital figure
53 Former East German secret police
55 Tubes in the kitchen
56 Tale
57 Marvel Comics heroes
58 Jeanne d'Arc et al.: Abbr.
59 Gumbo component
60 Without ice
61 Relig. training ground
64 Company in Italy?

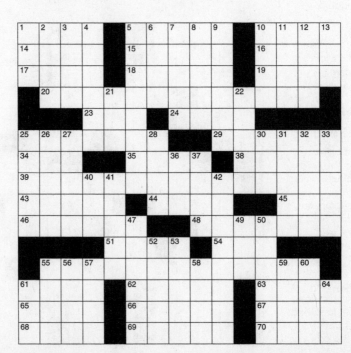

by William I. Johnston

ACROSS

1. ___ d'Or (award at Cannes)
6. Mimic
9. To ___ (without exception)
13. Eero Saarinen's architect father
14. Actor Jannings
15. 1953 Leslie Caron film
16. God, to a Muslim
17. Wine valley in California
18. Skin lotion ingredient
19. "The Little Foxes" playwright
22. Shoebox marking
23. Sign on a door
24. Top-notch
25. Haleakala National Park site
27. ___ Jima
29. Cart part
32. Lennon's widow
33. Hull projection
37. Nightgown wearer of rhyme
41. In good health
42. Part of many e-mail addresses
43. Nancy Drew author Carolyn
44. Comic Philips
45. "Boy, am I tired!"
47. "Murphy Brown" bar owner
50. Cabbage's cousin
52. Buddy
55. City whose language uses only the 12 letters found in this puzzle
59. Hawkeye's home
60. ". . . hear ___ drop"
61. Lousy car
62. Shade of blue
63. Brother
64. Syrup flavor
65. Carol
66. Compass dir.
67. "Gil Blas" novelist Lesage

DOWN

1. Artist Rembrandt ___
2. Kate's TV roommate
3. Northern French city
4. Ground-up corn
5. Designed for all grades
6. "___ and the Night Visitors"
7. Oil conduit
8. Israeli airline
9. San Antonio landmark
10. La Scala's city
11. Unaccompanied
12. Never, in Nürnberg
14. Boredom
20. Kwik-E-Mart owner on "The Simpsons"
21. ___-tzu
25. Whimper
26. The Greatest
28. "Holy cow!"
29. http:// follower
30. TV's "___ Haw"
31. Snaky fish
32. Deep-frying need
33. Sensed
34. Barely make, with "out"
35. German article
36. "Crooklyn" director
38. Hasty escape
39. Regard
40. '50s prez
44. "Xanadu" grp.
45. Coin sound
46. When repeated, a snicker
47. Receiver button
48. Actor Mandel
49. Fully
51. Dress cut
52. Argentine plain
53. Garlicky mayonnaise
54. Sheets and stuff
56. Crippled
57. Soprano Gluck
58. Prosperity
59. Actor Ziering

by Peter Gordon

ACROSS
1 Pepsi or RC
5 Kuwaiti ruler
9 Stares open-mouthed
14 Birthstone after sapphire
15 Cheese nibblers
16 "My Fair Lady" lady
17 Courtroom figures
20 Winding road shape
21 Loch ___ monster
22 Lassos
23 Proofreader's mark
24 Tilling tools
25 Like fishers' hooks
28 Top 40 songs
29 Poem of praise
32 Command
33 Indian dress
34 Hertz rival
35 Ida Lupino, e.g.
38 Lawyers' charges
39 Topic of gossip
40 Because
41 Like octogenarians
42 Squalid neighborhood
43 Time of the year
44 Ooze
45 Candies that burn the mouth
46 "Is that your final ___?"
49 D.C. bigwigs
50 Low digit?
53 Last governor of New Netherland
56 Wear away
57 ___ Stanley Gardner
58 Company V.I.P.
59 Scattered, as seed
60 Requirement
61 Action before blowing out the candles

DOWN
1 Make do
2 Any symphony
3 Places for experiments
4 Entirely
5 Hosted
6 Central spot
7 Desserts that give chills
8 Striped official
9 Bottled spirits
10 Actors Robert and Alan
11 Artist Mondrian
12 Book after II Chronicles
13 Back talk
18 Recent med school graduate
19 Arousing
23 Parts with thorns
24 Ulysses S. Grant's real first name
25 Successful, in Variety
26 The Little Mermaid's name
27 Ran without moving
28 Sheik's bevy
29 Kilns
30 Music to do the hustle to
31 German industrial city
33 Ab strengthener
34 Opera songs
36 Edmonton N.H.L. team
37 Sleeping sickness carrier
42 Become enraged
43 Figured out
44 Ingmar Bergman, e.g.
45 According to ___
46 Earth rulers in a 1968 film
47 Imperious Roman
48 Put away
49 Like 24-karat gold
50 Hack's vehicle
51 Singles
52 Write on metal
54 Sawbuck
55 Make a seam

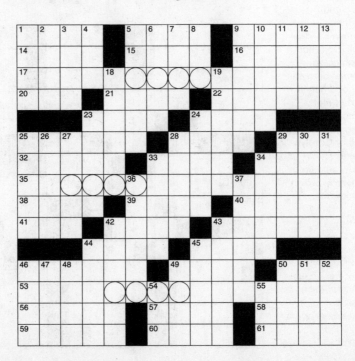

by Peter Gordon

A certain letter of the alphabet appears in this puzzle exactly 21 times. When you have finished solving, find and connect these letters to get an appropriate design.

ACROSS

1 Smelling salts container
5 Mooch
8 Learn in passing
14 Weaving together
16 Add
17 1955 musical version of "Cinderella"
19 Cowpunch's moniker
20 Tree whose winged seeds look like tiny canoe paddles
21 It's an honor
22 Northern Indians
24 Low ___
26 More cunning
29 Grandkids, to grandparents
30 Philosophical
32 Carlo who wrote "Christ Stopped at Eboli"
33 Roadside sign
35 Not very engaging
37 Side dish, for short
38 One who delivers papers
42 How Miss Piggy refers to herself
43 Delicacy at a state dinner?
44 Urchin's home
45 Frequently
47 Hideaway
49 Old West gunman Jack
53 Los ___
55 Fragrant ring
56 Brad Pitt thriller
57 Resulted (from)
59 Superhuman ability
61 Cockpit abbr.
62 Mission of a sort
66 Morning music
67 Wordsworth, for one
68 Casserole crust
69 Private
70 Hammock holder

DOWN

1 Checked for accuracy
2 Be essential (to)
3 Greek princess
4 Time difference
5 Judge's no-no
6 Never expressed, as tears
7 Some British imports
8 Portraitist Frans
9 Long stories
10 Revolt
11 Stay on death row
12 Start of a long-distance call
13 N.Y.C. artery, with "the"
15 Person of grace and dignity
18 Prompts grave thoughts in
23 As a result
25 Fairy-tale monster
27 By any chance
28 Set up
31 They have wedges
34 It makes an impression
36 More fancy
38 Knit shirt
39 City in central Ecuador
40 Balance
41 Sheltered spot
42 Bad start?
46 Clawed
48 Carpentry tool
50 Embodiment of a god
51 Computer key
52 Main order
54 Old Italian coppers
58 Grasped
60 Stay away from
62 She-demon
63 Lord's Prayer beginning
64 ___-pitch
65 Replayed shot

by Patrick Berry

ACROSS

1 A ___ of pheasants
8 A ___ of geese
14 Good sign on a sales chart
15 Golf ball distances
16 Like some old coats
17 Harmonizes
18 Swarm member
19 Extraterrestrial, e.g.
20 Fishes for
25 Marks along some swimming pools
28 Former U.S. defense acronym
31 Waste (away)
33 Big bird
34 An ___ of larks
36 Carpenter's groove
37 Certain records or cars
38 Pal, colloquially
39 Man
40 Electrical units
41 A ___ of owls
43 Social
44 Court attorneys, e.g.
45 Crude shelter
46 It's mind-boggling
48 Jabber
50 Noted Discovery passenger, 1998
52 Mouth, in slang
56 One of the sacraments
58 It's hard to see through
61 Fixed
62 Not perfectly round
63 A ___ of crows
64 A ___ of woodpeckers

DOWN

1 Town
2 Certain tournament
3 Arthur Ashe's alma mater
4 What you may call it?
5 Jardiniere
6 Planning time
7 Newsman Koppel
8 Some estate workers
9 More Village-y
10 Kind of work
11 Common mixers
12 Author Harper
13 Twisty curve
15 Trucker's spot
21 Lizards, old-style
22 Tide competitor
23 Overnight gear
24 It might help you get a leg up
26 Porcupine, for one
27 Original "Star Trek" role
28 Composed
29 Lumberjacks
30 Person on a trail
32 Factory worker
35 Part of L.A.
36 Obstruct
39 Broad
41 Member of an annual team
42 Nest egg, for short
44 Fine, in France
47 Thymus, e.g.
49 Body of good conduct
51 "Old Uncle" in a Stephen Foster tune
53 Endured, with "out"
54 Mathematician Turing
55 Hit
56 Actress Dawber
57 Big bird
58 Capsule
59 Suffix with elect
60 Rejections

by John Scott Marrone

ACROSS

1 Queen's land
6 Data card debris
10 Fast-food option
14 Greens
15 Learning style
16 Discordant
17 West Indian parent?
20 Dangerous situation
21 Pitch
22 Part of N.E.A.: Abbr.
23 "Kiss me as if it were the last time" speaker
25 Telephone part
28 Fruit cake?
33 Draw upon
34 Lap dog
35 Buy in a hurry
36 SeaWorld resident
38 Street shadower
40 Thit and thas?
41 Dangerous pronouncements
43 Medieval or modern weapon
45 Tough cleaner
46 Laugh on a bike?
48 Come clean, with "up"
49 New York congresswoman ___ Lowey
50 Some time ago
52 Most respectful (of)
55 Earning position
60 Art form in Quebec?
62 Carbon compound
63 1960s singer with the Del Satins
64 Ubangi's outlet
65 Dress (up)
66 Itsy-bitsy
67 Supplicant's supporters

DOWN

1 Army E-6: Abbr.
2 Mata ___
3 Spirit
4 Got together
5 Did sums
6 Shore dinner appetizer
7 Jolly response
8 Loss of muscle coordination
9 Clinton, e.g.: Abbr.
10 Buccaneer's place
11 California town east of Santa Barbara
12 Ready and willing
13 Kind of tradition
18 Comic Lenny
19 Armand of "The Marrying Man"
24 They may hang in the balance: Abbr.
25 Like some jobs
26 Kitty ___ (mistress in Irish history)
27 Get strong again
29 Seat of Dallas County, Alabama
30 Computer logo
31 They barely keep their heads above water
32 Parts of chapels
34 Less apt to wait one's turn
37 Have good intentions
39 Reddish-brown
42 China's Sun ___-sen
44 Like some chairs
47 Pro Bowl site
48 Eat
51 Striking noise
52 "___ Three Lives"
53 Jumping a line, e.g.
54 Concern for an M.P.
56 This may follow words of wisdom
57 Rooster site, maybe
58 Result of honing
59 Golden Triangle country
61 Chi. clock setting

by Manny Nosowsky

62

ACROSS

1 Lady abroad
5 With 50-Down, steak go-with
10 With 68-Across, fish filet go-with
14 Wedding parties?: Abbr.
15 Water, for one
16 Tel ___
17 Psyche components
18 Fix, as a hitch
19 Unnerve
20 "Yep" negator
21 Behind closed doors
23 Drug-free
25 Well-founded
29 He-man
33 With 44-Across, hot sandwich go-with
34 Like waves on a shoreline
37 It's on the St. Lawrence River: Abbr.
38 Hilarious . . . or a hint to this puzzle's theme
42 Brown, in ads
43 Passed
44 See 33-Across
47 Closed tight
51 White-knuckle
54 Make a ship stop by facing the wind
55 Newscast lead
59 Drift ___
60 Airline rarity, nowadays
63 "May ___ your order?"
64 Bob Dylan's first wife and the title of a song about her
65 Makeover
66 Stinky
67 Dirty magazines and such
68 See 10-Across
69 See 1-Down
70 Neither good nor bad

DOWN

1 With 69-Across, burger go-with
2 Treat splendidly
3 One saying "I do"
4 Letters before Liberty or Constitution
5 Sprung (from)
6 x, y and z
7 Toy sometimes seen on a beach
8 Order
9 Big name in balers
10 Unisex dress
11 Female gametes
12 1995 showbiz biography by C. David Heymann
13 December 31, e.g.
21 Harden
22 Musician Brian
24 Breezed through
26 One of a series of joint Soviet/U.S. space satellites
27 Dragged out
28 Suffix with absorb
30 Shake, in a way
31 Cable inits. since 1979
32 Albino in "The Da Vinci Code"
35 Police target
36 Jazzy James
38 Something to take in a car
39 Fred Astaire's "___ This a Lovely Day"
40 The Beeb is seen on it
41 "The very ___!"
42 The Rams of the Atlantic 10 Conf.
45 2003 #2 hit for Lil Jon and the East Side Boyz
46 ___-Cat
48 Go-getter
49 Womb
50 See 5-Across
52 Spruce (up)
53 Perfume ingredient
56 1955 Oscar nominee for "Mr. Hulot's Holiday"
57 Tex's neighbor to the north
58 Some wines
59 Partner, informally, with "the"
61 Underwater cave dweller
62 Oral health org.
64 Draft org.

by Lucy Gardner Anderson

ACROSS

1 Related on the mother's side
6 Card game with the 13 spades laid out
10 Unadorned
14 Expensive watch
15 Fine horse
16 "That's ___!"
17 Dessert made with pineapple
19 Deli order
20 Some facial features
21 Out-and-out
22 Like some golf balls
23 Six, in Tuscany
24 Phone trio
25 Body of work
27 Was considered special
29 Flip
31 Strauss's "___ Heldenleben"
32 Play stations?
34 Produced
36 Alliance
39 Car opener?
41 Gridiron move
42 Left ventricle attachment
44 Hunk
46 William, to Diana
47 Partied, so to speak
49 Sentences
52 Very soon
54 Chamber worker?: Abbr.
55 Part of i.o.u.
57 Old ___, Conn.
58 "___ letter" (office order)
61 War maker
62 Wild goat
63 Title song of a Duke Ellington album
65 Gérard Depardieu work
66 One may be turning
67 Make merry
68 Red army?
69 Caltech grad: Abbr.
70 Be economical with

DOWN

1 Explodes
2 More of a buttinsky
3 Concert pianist de Larrocha
4 Nugent and Turner
5 Letters ending a PC code file name
6 See 35-Down
7 "I smell ___!"
8 Shed item
9 Shakespearean fairy
10 African language
11 Soap ingredient
12 Rental stables
13 They get you nowhere
18 Where they say "G'day!"
24 Riviera vista
26 Cosmo staff
28 Social grace
29 Yo-yoing
30 This, to Jorge
33 Like some drink orders
35 With 6-Down, a logician's phrase
36 Vatican attraction
37 Zoo, so to speak
38 Gargoyle, e.g.
40 Like native llamas
43 Ripen
45 Charged item
48 Eightfold
50 Doctor in an H. G. Wells title
51 Workout wear
53 Battle of the ___
54 One who'll put you in stitches?
56 Name on an atomizer
59 ___ impasse
60 King ___
61 Competent
64 Sedative, informally

by Elizabeth C. Gorski

ACROSS

1 Go out
6 Understands
10 Put away
14 Big can producer
15 Door sign
16 Topological shapes
17 Finishing school enrollees
18 Danish toy company
19 Election losers
20 Carried too much?
23 Shoe part
25 Red Sox legend Williams
26 Kind of trip
27 Leopard, e.g.
28 Heroic tales
31 Construction element
33 Heroic tale
35 Strenuous class
36 Ike's W.W. II command
37 Quick, strong alcoholic drinks?
42 It may be positive or negative
43 Sass
44 "Pygmalion" playwright
46 ___ acid
49 Baseballer noted for bon mots
51 Bank offering, for short
52 Freight weight
53 Île ___ Marie
55 Modern Persians
57 Slap shots for Jagr or Lemieux?
61 Unwritten
62 Part of a horse's pedigree
63 Smell
66 Appropriately named Colorado county
67 Smell
68 Wild throw, e.g.
69 1950s P.M.
70 Top-of-the-hour radio offering
71 Spiteful

DOWN

1 Hang back
2 Ivy Leaguer
3 Clever verse
4 Latin for "I roll"
5 Stands in a studio
6 Shower soaps
7 Office honcho
8 Ballet wear
9 Non-P.C. garb
10 Desist
11 Something put on the spot?
12 Former Sandinista leader
13 Sagacity
21 President who was also a sportscaster
22 Bunker matriarch
23 Clinch
24 Refreshers, you might say
29 Swindle
30 Sufficient
32 Derisive reception
34 Gab
36 Zing
38 Tightenable loop
39 Yes or no follower
40 Academic types
41 Bombay wear
45 Used to be
46 Not out
47 Tied up, in a way
48 As a precaution
49 Next to
50 Come to light
54 Whom Holyfield KO'd, 11/9/96
56 Capital on the Gulf of Guinea
58 Hate group
59 Rooster's cry
60 His's partner
64 "___ so fast!"
65 Taste

by Richard Chisholm

65

ACROSS

1 Moolah
5 Unwarm welcome
9 Lonely heights
13 Zone
14 9th-century founder of the Russian monarchy
15 Help in ways one shouldn't
16 Musical with the song "The Night They Invented Champagne"
17 Stradivarius's teacher
18 Forearm bone
19 "Jeopardy!" format
22 Profess
23 O
24 Ship that's remembered
27 ___-blond
30 1960s catchword
33 Electrician's unit
34 Take-home
37 *
38 Sales agents
40 Leaf opening
41 Word with wheat or missile
42 "Gunfight at the O.K. Corral" role
43 Hardly tiptoes
45 Antique
46 Warrior's weapon
48 ___ out a win
49 Rigid
51 They're found all along the line: Abbr.
53 500 sheets
55 Famous comedy team à la "Jeopardy!"
62 Theater award
63 Soft glows
64 Met song
65 Hood's beneficiaries, with "the"
66 Begin
67 Sideways look
68 Hankerings
69 Command's site
70 Forest growth

DOWN

1 Dotty
2 Land of Killarney
3 Runners
4 Made in ___
5 U2 tour and film à la "Jeopardy!"
6 Country under longtime U.N. sanctions
7 In ___ (as placed)
8 Downhill racer
9 Degree of strain
10 A must-do
11 City near Sparks
12 Ollie's partner
14 Not common
20 Not odd
21 Just enough to wet one's lips
24 Conventions
25 ___ o' livin'
26 Rich Little forte
28 Scare
29 Kitchen product à la "Jeopardy!"
31 Phones
32 Wear
35 Computer key
36 Bark
39 Paints like Pollock
44 Wild guess
47 1979 film "Norma ___"
50 Make a mummy
52 Not just trim
54 N.C.A.A. tournament division
55 Reproduce
56 Woodwind instrument
57 String instrument
58 Spoken
59 Modern ice cream flavor
60 Makes a bow
61 Sailors

by Steven Dorfman

ACROSS

1. It involves a lot of back-and-forth
7. Deeply connected with
14. Goes up and down
16. Subject of the Brest-Litovsk treaty, 1918
17. Tiara
18. Is uncertain to, briefly
19. Regal letters
20. "With a wink and ___"
22. Like worker bees
23. Cardinal O'Connor's successor
25. Small branch
27. What's ___ . . .
28. Shred
30. Lawn starter
31. Nervous time, maybe
32. "The Maltese Falcon" actress
34. ___ mater (brain cover)
36. Suffix with cannon
37. Camping gear
40. Bawl
42. Dot follower
43. Value system
46. With 9-Down, something to feel
47. "That's awesome!"
49. Fortune teller, maybe
51. Grammarian's bugaboo
53. Certain convertibles
55. Incompletely
56. Enjoying an activity
58. Social group
60. "Car Talk" network
61. Repair shop amenities
63. Part of a rock band
65. Glass-enclosed porches
66. Bach's "Pilgrimage," for one
67. Unwelcome handouts
68. Minneapolis's county

DOWN

1. Good watchdog
2. Bulldog's place
3. "If you play your cards right"
4. Spanish bear
5. Babushka
6. Actress Verdon and others
7. No-goodnik
8. Giving the go-ahead
9. See 46-Across
10. Old Testament figure who prophesied Nineveh's fall
11. Copied, in a way
12. Intimidate
13. Needle holder
15. Old telegram punctuation
21. Dozing
24. Bonkers
26. "Gotcha"
29. Nov. runner
33. Early touring car
35. A Warner Bros. brother
36. Sheikhs' guests, maybe
38. Switch add-on
39. Part of a long-distance company's 800 number
40. Army helicopter
41. Certain summer cottages
44. Tough guy
45. Go for the gold
46. Emergency situation
48. Canadian capital?
50. American turtle
52. Like most music
53. Take off
54. Vaughan of jazz
57. Yesterday, in Italy
59. Air
62. Trans-Atlantic carrier
64. K2 is one: Abbr.

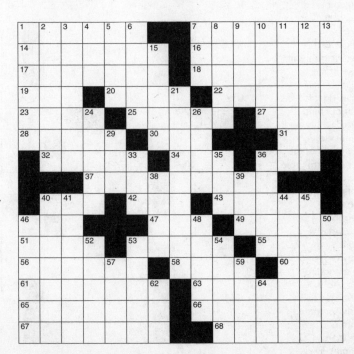

by Manny Nosowsky

ACROSS
1 "Gee whillikers!"
5 Deviate
9 Terra ___
14 Judge
15 Switch ending
16 Thai or Taiwanese
17 Suffix with fabric
18 Valley girl?
19 Mad
20 Alaska
23 High-ranking clergyman
24 ___ Fables
28 "Snow White and the Seven Dwarfs"
31 Biblical tower site
34 Home, informally
35 A, in Aachen
36 Dumbfounded
37 "___ say . . ."
39 Judge's seat
40 Org. governing two conferences
41 Japanese soup
42 Funny hitting sounds
43 The Clermont
47 Aloft
48 Supporter
52 What 20-, 28- and 43-Across each turned into
55 Cassette contents
58 Goes kaput
59 How many a product is advertised
60 Idolize
61 ". . . or ___!"
62 Lone Star State sch.
63 Windblown soil
64 Famed loch
65 Prepare a salad

DOWN
1 Hold
2 Horse opera
3 "Uncle Tom's Cabin" writer
4 Proclaimed
5 Grazing lands for gnus
6 Up
7 Massage deeply
8 It can be used to walk the dog
9 Ultraliberals
10 Arbitrary parental "explanation"
11 Eve's beginning
12 Month after avril
13 Additionally
21 Stairwell item
22 Catch, as a bronco
25 Western New York town
26 Toy piano sound
27 Does a film editor's job
29 ___ the line
30 Thus far
31 Canada's ___ National Park
32 Terrible
33 Mideastern dancer's asset
37 Burn lightly
38 Donkey
39 Three-fingered saluter
41 1820 White House residents
42 Group
44 Princeton team
45 Fixate (on)
46 Scoundrels
49 Fifty minutes past the hour
50 Adlai's running mate
51 Answers an invitation
53 Gulf of ___ (entrance to the Red Sea)
54 Mah-jongg piece
55 Prince in the comics, for short
56 Altar declaration
57 Female hare

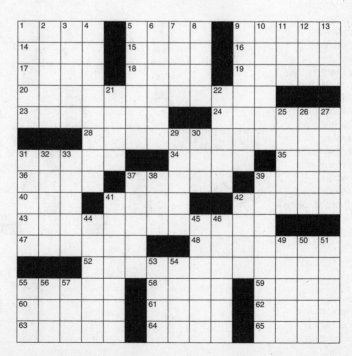

by Patrick Merrell

ACROSS

1 Rich, raisiny cake
5 Knuckler alternative
10 Court helper
14 Work in the media
15 Jazz pianist Marsalis
16 Museo work
17 Fathers' robes
18 Cheery
19 Broadway luminary?
20 It rises in Lake Victoria
21 ___ X
22 Throws off
24 In-line skate part
26 Start of a simple game
27 "___ a perfumed sea . . .": Poe
28 Synchronize anew
32 Commode component
36 Flap
38 Ride in a shuttle
39 Tale of Vikings, perhaps
40 Cartoon aficionado's purchase
41 Comment after the fog clears
42 Manual consultants
44 Fish of the genus Electrophorus
45 Cold war ammunition?
46 She ranks
48 ___-Pitch
50 In addition
51 Mess up at a critical moment
56 He stopped smoking cigars in 1985
59 Hockey shutout
60 Hockey position
61 Symbol of life
62 Gives the nod to
64 One-two connector
65 In ___ (even)
66 Caribbean port
67 Footnote word
68 Tennis miss
69 Rounded end
70 Revealing work of art?

DOWN

1 Dangerous pitch
2 Unrehearsed
3 Job site?
4 One way to be lost
5 Former Windsor in-law, informally
6 "Star Trek" peoples
7 Talk on the street
8 Foil material
9 Hoosier university
10 Jailbird's burden
11 Belgian balladeer
12 Missouri's ally, once
13 Desires
23 Market corrections
25 Seoul soldier
28 Big wheel's wheels
29 Plus
30 Offed
31 Look at
32 Muddles
33 Possessive, e.g.
34 S-curve
35 Be in charge
37 River to the North Sea
43 Nostradamus, for one
45 Saturate
47 Street game
49 Relax
51 College in Crete, Neb.
52 "What Is Man?" essayist
53 Caste member
54 Through
55 It may follow the national anthem
56 "Slither" star, 1973
57 ___ meridiem
58 Little play
63 Comical lawman

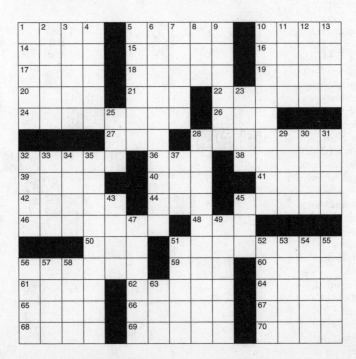

by Robert H. Wolfe

ACROSS

1 Subject for Ovid
5 Go well together
9 "Splendor in the Grass" screenwriter
13 Obviously surprised
14 North Carolina county named for an early governor
15 Hand-colored frames
16 "I'm not gonna stand in their way"
17 Like some diamonds
19 Crunchy bowlful
21 Followed
22 Skirt
24 New Deal inits.
25 Grid
28 With 37- and 43-Across, one who takes after dad
33 Faraway
34 Sugar suffixes
35 Piniella of baseball
36 Bygone prison
37 See 28-Across or 4-Down
38 Just below 90
40 Tauromachian chant
41 Jacob ___ Park, in Queens
42 River of Orléans
43 See 28-Across
46 Dove competitor
47 Fair-hiring inits.
48 "All I gotta do ___ naturally" (Beatles lyric)
50 Certain red
54 City near South Bend
58 Beat around the bend?
60 Bacall's love
61 1847 novel set on Tahiti
62 Norwegian saint
63 Uniform shade
64 Number 10 on a table
65 "Ode to the Confederate Dead" poet Allen ___
66 TV's warrior princess

DOWN

1 Sun, to skin
2 Spy ___ Hari
3 Undeveloped expanse
4 With 37-Across and 38-Down, step taken after an airline accident
5 Kenyan tribesman
6 Atty.'s title
7 Out of business
8 Hot spots
9 One in the pole position?
10 Thin part
11 Sticker
12 Founded: Abbr.
13 Afr. country
18 Sitarist Shankar
20 Bagel shop order
23 Brightly colored pullover garment
25 Squinting Mr.
26 Have ___ in the conversation
27 Like most bathrooms
29 Bee chasers
30 Man with Stan, familiarly
31 Rare trick takers
32 Things useful when put in a box
34 Ear-related
38 See 4-Down
39 Cabin brightener
41 Plant plight
44 Source of hope?
45 Nightly TV star beginning 5/25/92
46 Berkeley campus, for short
49 Start court proceedings?
50 Masked critter
51 Journalist Brit
52 Langston Hughes poem
53 "To Live and Die ___"
55 Opposin'
56 Racehorse ___ Ridge
57 It gives support in sport
59 Clean a plate

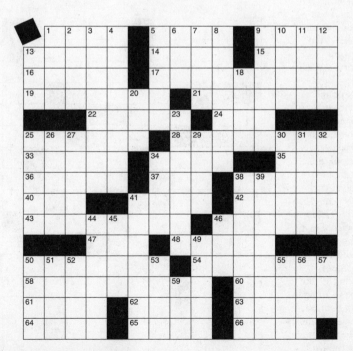

by Patrick Merrell

ACROSS

1 How ham may be served in a sandwich
6 Popular kitchen wrap
11 Tiny bit, as of hair cream
14 Oscar Mayer product
15 Skip to the altar
16 Billy Joel's "___ to Extremes"
17 The Bard
19 Judges administer it
20 Hammed it up
21 Thick urban air condition
23 City where "Ulysses" is set
26 Item carried by a dog walker
28 Columbus sch.
29 "Mona Lisa" features that "follow" the viewer
32 Years, to Cicero
33 Large bays
35 PIN points
37 Concept
40 Shopping ___
41 Theme of this puzzle
42 Shopping ___
43 ___ Romeo (Italian car)
44 G.M. car, once
45 Birth-related
46 Ancient South American
48 Meditative exercises
50 Spanish "that"
51 Lions and tigers and bears
54 Stage comments to the audience
56 Alternative
57 Safes

60 Turncoat
61 Very scary
66 Spanish cheer
67 Synthetic fiber
68 Continental money
69 Neither's partner
70 Mexican money
71 Gaucho's rope

DOWN

1 Delivery room docs, for short
2 "I don't think so"
3 Major TV brand
4 Bumpkin
5 Foes
6 Equinox mo.
7 Out of the wind, at sea
8 All of them lead to Rome, they say
9 Tax mo.

10 Liam of "Schindler's List"
11 Run-down
12 Staring
13 Shady garden spot
18 Major TV brand
22 One of the friends on "Friends"
23 Bedrock belief
24 Commonplace
25 Waver of a red cape
27 Throw, as dice
30 Count's counterpart
31 Pore over
34 Projecting rim on a pipe
36 Japanese soup
38 Wipe out
39 World book

41 Pillow filler
45 Not as nice
47 Drive-in restaurant server
49 Grand party
51 Element with the symbol B
52 Author Calvino
53 Lesser of two ___
55 It's debatable
58 Suffix with buck
59 Big coffee holders
62 With 64-Down, reply to "Am too!"
63 Tax adviser's recommendation, for short
64 See 62-Down
65 Fed. property overseer

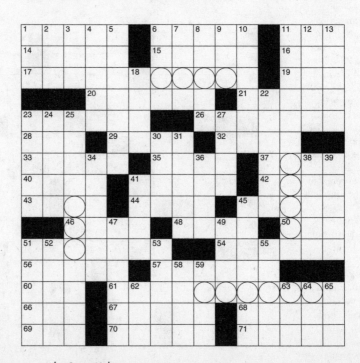

by Steve Kahn

ACROSS

1 Hawthorne's birthplace
6 Herbert who won a Pulitzer for "The People's Choice"
10 It's a matter of opinion
14 City west of Daytona Beach
15 Crème ___ crème
16 Exotic vacation spot
17 Fume
18 Canal exploration devices
20 This once was sufficient
22 Community program
23 Park ___ (N.Y.C. locale)
25 Lunchtime
27 Name fit for a king?
28 Connecting point
29 Apparition
34 Shock jock's overseer, for short
35 Does simple math
36 Straight dope
37 ". . . men in ___"
39 Huey, Dewey, Louie, Donald and Daisy
42 Magical opening
43 Dr. ___ ("A Beautiful Mind" role)
45 "Of course, Jorge!"
47 Trash collector
48 Unencumbered by
50 Get ___ (share the rewards of)
51 Blood-curdling scream
52 Raise
54 Transp. network
55 "What a Girl Wants" singer, 1999
59 Motorcade V.I.P.: Abbr.
61 Trade association?
63 Key material
66 "Born Free" lioness
67 Slaughter the slugger
68 Portia's role on "Ally McBeal"
69 Negotiation's end
70 Tailor-made
71 Lock

DOWN

1 Blubber
2 Prince of a guy
3 "The dog ate my homework," e.g.
4 Vivacity
5 Raphael subject
6 Fuss and bother
7 Do some planning before taking action
8 For all to hear
9 Followers of Bob Marley's music
10 Wind up on stage?
11 Sobriquet for Haydn
12 What a conductor conducts: Abbr.
13 Gossip
19 Underground chamber
21 Long-crested bird
23 Bow-wow
24 Missile's course
26 Weirdo
30 A Gershwin
31 Part of an all-weather shoe
32 Self-consoling words
33 "That's just what I needed!"
38 Quilters' do
40 Avoiding spitballs, say
41 Classic Marx Brothers flick
44 Viscount, e.g.
46 Available from the publisher
49 Burgundy brothers
53 One of the Horae
55 Tucked in
56 Fast-moving wind
57 ___ Minor
58 Type type: Abbr.
60 Present opener?
62 Form 1040 ID
64 Literary inits.
65 "You rang?"

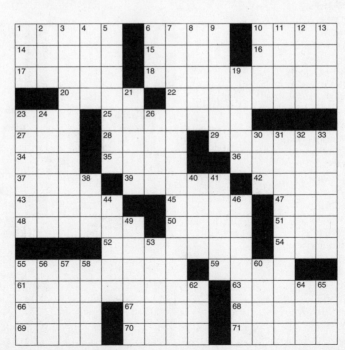

by Elizabeth C. Gorski

72

ACROSS

1 Tackle's protection
5 Indian silk center
10 Letters for a religious scholar
13 Outlet output: Abbr.
14 Funny cars might burn it
15 Curb, with "in"
17 Sports car, familiarly
18 More blue?
19 "Argghh!"
20 What fall traditionally brings
23 Intoxicating
24 Restaurant posting
25 Part of a school's Web site name
26 Shore soarer
27 "Sprechen ___ Deutsch?"
30 Annie or Dondi, of the comics
32 Collectors' goals
34 Hydrocarbon suffixes
37 Staff members: Abbr.
38 Ones responding to 20-Across
41 "Git!"
44 Mess overseers: Abbr.
45 Bounders
49 Easy marks
51 Old White House inits.
53 "Nope"
54 Suffix with human
55 Luxury
58 Screwball
60 What 38-Across might take
64 Sportswear brand
65 Shot from a tee

66 Word before and after "à"
67 Back-to-school mo.
68 Like some shoes and drinks
69 Actresses Balin and Claire
70 1965 Ursula Andress film
71 ___ nous
72 Cig. boxes

DOWN

1 Beauties
2 "None missing"
3 Not giving in one bit
4 Throw hot water on
5 Pro's foe
6 "Your majesty"
7 Drang's counterpart
8 Am I, doubled
9 Rita of "West Side Story"
10 Track race
11 Sly laughs
12 Patronized, as a restaurant
16 One result of a perfect game
21 Fleur-de-___
22 Presences
28 It makes "adverb" an adjective
29 Cuts off
31 Infinitesimal division of a min.
33 Did laps, say
35 Grade A item
36 Clockmaker Thomas
39 Louvre pyramid architect

40 Tilde's shape, loosely
41 Pooh-poohs
42 Spicy ingredients
43 Leader in a holiday song
46 As old as the hills
47 Upper Midwesterner
48 Social problem
50 Sit on it
52 Pan Am competitor
56 S. C. Johnson wrap
57 Boot
59 Cobwebby area
61 Monitor's measure
62 Assert
63 Turn over

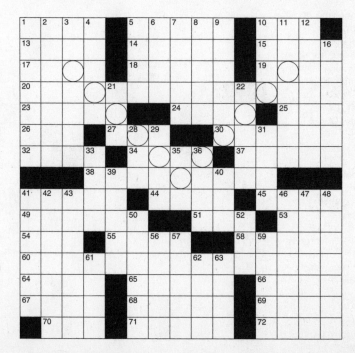

by Patrick Merrell

ACROSS

1 "Ignorance ___ excuse"
5 Large quantity of writing
10 Live folk album of 1968
14 Annual prize named after a Canadian governor general
16 Visited
17 1985 sci-fi rerun?
19 They might be chained
20 Constellation near Scorpius
21 ___-la
22 Undercoat
24 New spouse's acquisitions, maybe
26 Hippodrome events
27 That girl
28 Not in
29 Bach's "Air ___ G String"
30 Dug in
31 Seek help
32 1990 sci-fi rerun?
37 Decide
38 Pot addition
39 "Six Feet Under" network
42 ___ art (text graphics)
45 Collared one
46 Singer McLachlan
48 Like an owl's eyes
50 Budweiser offerings
51 See 22-Down
52 Not originals of letters, for short
53 Après-ski beverage
54 1983 sci-fi rerun?
59 Storybook meanie
60 Carnivores
61 Egg container
62 It's placed at the counter
63 ___ the kill

DOWN

1 Suffix with expert
2 Sailors' passage: Abbr.
3 Like some knots
4 Punctual
5 Make allusions (to)
6 Scrutinizes
7 "Alas" in Augsburg
8 Change dramatically
9 Puffball emanation
10 "Don't ___!"
11 Odd pages
12 Picks up
13 Part way to scoring
15 Angler's collection
18 Click and Clack, the ___ Brothers
22 With 51-Across, for the nonce
23 Published
24 Dessert eaten with a spoon
25 Palm starch
27 ___-Anne-de-Beaupré, Québec
30 Do one's part?
31 Cave denizen
33 Hi's partner
34 Each
35 Court call
36 Loom
40 Keep out
41 Exclamations of surprise
42 Shout on the set
43 Heavy hitter
44 Rising stars
45 Drive up the wall
46 Pelvic bones
47 Rabbitlike rodent
49 Ordinary Joe
50 Extrovert's opposite
53 Homing pigeon's home
55 Black
56 Furbys, once
57 Distinctive time
58 Q–U link

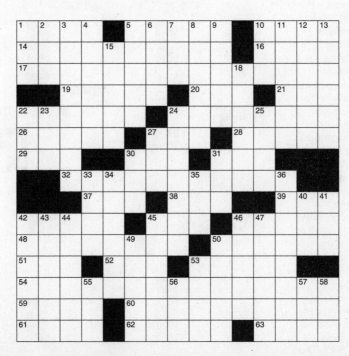

by Jerry E. Rosman

ACROSS

1 Computer insert
5 Rib
10 Peach ___
14 Campagna di ___ (geographical region)
15 Lets up
16 Beggary
17 Hospital numbers?
19 Singer from Hawaii
20 Umpire's call
21 Square
23 "The Lord of the Rings" actress
26 Tip off
27 W.W. II hero
29 Slow mover
31 Bliss
34 Subcompact
35 Court call
38 One of six found in this puzzle
41 Directional suffix
42 Middling marks
43 Period from opening day to the playoffs
44 Came to be
46 Tenn.'s Cumberland ___
47 Prepares potatoes in a way
51 They block passes
54 Player at home
56 Capital on the Delaware
59 Moolah
60 Turn off unneeded lights, e.g.
63 Choose
64 Moves round and round
65 "Do the Right Thing" pizzeria
66 Retreats
67 Make ___ of
68 ___' Pea (Popeye's kid)

DOWN

1 Ho-hum
2 Hebrides isle
3 Place where everybody knows everybody
4 Carnival staple
5 Minuscule
6 Studio items
7 "___ recall . . ."
8 Org. that protects investors
9 In ___ (really)
10 Pioneer geneticist
11 Sierra ___
12 Biblical epic
13 Begin using
18 Main subj. of a constitution
22 Bag
24 All together
25 It may delay things
27 Adjust
28 Roman road
30 Polit. wild cards
32 If
33 New-___
35 Final provocation
36 Harrow rival
37 Perfect marks
39 13 popes, so far
40 Docility
45 Records
47 Like Batman and Robin
48 Past the expiration date
49 Ancient abductee
50 Sets up
52 Lock
53 Nothing abroad
55 Greek peak
57 Eye
58 Wall St. landmark
61 Convenience store convenience
62 Go (for)

by Richard Chisholm

ACROSS

1 Dark cloud
5 Twelve Oaks neighbor
9 1994 Nobel Peace Prize sharer
14 Pope from 440 to 461
15 Drew on
16 Get past
17 Composer Khachaturian
18 Not opt.
19 It'll keep you up
20 Mali dancewear?
23 Pal of Roo
24 Itty bit
25 Boss's Day mo.
28 East ___, Conn.
30 Represent
32 Biblical verb
36 Response to a Nebraskan's gag?
38 On the horizon, maybe
41 Really steamed
42 Japanese plaything?
44 Hawaii's state bird
45 What 10's represent
46 Loaf parts
49 Rock's Nugent
50 One-third of a hat trick
52 Key with four sharps
57 Hawaiian doozy?
59 Raise the roof
62 Novelist Jaffe
63 Seed coat
64 Third of eight
65 Jenna or Barbara Bush
66 Relocate
67 Mandela's native tongue
68 "Now, about . . ."
69 Tram loads

DOWN

1 Home ___
2 Eagle's home
3 Like some good soil
4 Dance at a bar?
5 Holiday roast
6 Playing ___ (court activity)
7 Mass for the dead
8 Beef up
9 Airport convenience
10 Baseball family name
11 Popular brew, for short
12 Swearing-in words
13 ___ Percé
21 www address
22 Orem native
25 Grown-up
26 Comic Myron
27 Disgruntled player's demand
29 Mr. of mysteries
31 Comparison word
32 Jazz cat's command
33 "+" pole
34 Reprimanded gently
35 "Hey there!"
37 Boundless time
39 Hill where Jesus was crucified
40 Green tea type
43 Shows age, in a way
47 Presidential middle name
48 Mustangs' sch.
51 Trunk artery
53 9-Down company
54 "12 Angry Men" role
55 Antipasto morsel
56 Hoyle's listings
57 Primitive homes
58 Condo, e.g.
59 V-chip target
60 "Oh, sure!"
61 Conquistador's prize

by John Underwood

The New York Times
CROSSWORDS
SMART PUZZLES PRESENTED WITH STYLE

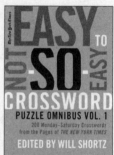

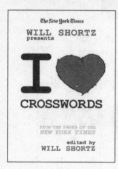
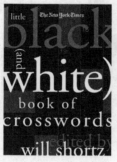
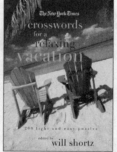

Available at your local bookstore or online at nytimes.com/nytstore.

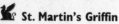 St. Martin's Griffin

1

```
A W L · L E S S · K A R A T S
S H H · A B U T · A M E N R A
H(E)A(T)W A V E · R A S T A S
E A S I L Y · V I A · T I C S
S T A L E · (B)E(A)(T)B A C K
· · S C I · N E A R · ·
(B)O(A)(T)S H O W · B A T O N S
E W E R · A L E N E · E N N E
D E S I L U · (B)O(L)(T)D O W N
· L I F T · S T R ·
· (B)O L(D)F A C E · E F L A T
C A L I · E G O · E A T E R Y
O R M O L U · (C)O L(D)S N A P
I R O N E R · O P I E · A B E
F E S S E S · A T A D · S Y S
```

2

```
W I N S · S I G M A · S P A M
A S E A · P L E A D · M A X I
L O W→ S R I N G S · A G E D
T U T O R I A L · · A R E ·
· R O U T E D · D O N T→E R
· · T A R · D A L I · B E E
P O L S · W A N E S · A R N
A B E · J O H N D O E · C I D
R E F · A M I T Y · · E K E S
E S T · P E T E · S Y N ·
R E→L A N E · U T A H A N
· · T O N · O P E R A H A T
T H O U · N O C→E D N O S E
A M O S · O N T A P · C O T E
D O Z E · D E A L S · E T Y M
```

3

```
P A C E · P L I E · L I M A
O L A V · A I N T · A N O N
E T T E · G E T A H*T A R T
M O O N S E T · S T I L E S
· N O P R O B · O N L Y ·
A D I D A S · A R N O · ·
R A N D R · T R E E · C P U
I V E S · H*O R T* · C O O S
D E T* · S U R E · R O C K S
· C O P A · T A L K E R
· B O O R · H O R S E T*
X R A Y E D · R I P S A W S
M A K E H*R O L L · L U A U
A C E S · I D O L · A C D C
S E N T · P E N S · W E E K
```

H* = HEADS; T* = TAILS

4

```
C A P O · [✊]B A C K · O F F[✊]
O P A L · S A R A N · A L U M
W E L D · D R A N O · T O G A
[✊]T O · C O M B A T · E G A D
· · O W S · · H A S S L E
S H A M A N · B L O T · ·
L A T E X · C O O L[✊]L U K E
A V I S · A R T I E · O N Y X
G E T A[✊]L E O N · N E U R O
· · I L E X · N E W M A N
F R E S N O · S E R · ·
O O L A · W O R K E D[✊]I N[✊]
R O A D · I N A I D · B A Y S
E T T A · N E M E A · A G R O
[✊]S E T · G L A D[✊]G O O N
```

5

```
B E T A · M A I N E · A R A B
O N E R · A R D O R · D E M O
S Y M B O L F O R S U L F U R
C A P O N · · R E E S E
· E R A · B E S T I R R E D
F A R E R · A G E E · ·
E R A T O · H O T N U M B E R
A C T U P · · N E E D Y
T H E M E S O N G · S T A I N
· · A R I A · H A U T E
R E F A S T E N S · O P T ·
A L I N E · · R H I N E
C O N T R A C T I O N O F I S
E P E E · H O A R D · R U N S
S E S S · A G R E E · S L O E
```

6

7

10 mistakes: Unsymmetrical grid; two 2-letter answers; LORE in the grid twice; ACROSS heading instead of DOWN; PUZZLE misspelled (56A); 50A clue out of order; two 13D clues; phony 37D clue; 47D answer repeated as its clue; puzzle number printed upside down.

8

9

10

11

J	U	I	C	Y		R	O	A	M		C	B	E	R
A	P	L	U	S		E	Z	R	A		H	I	R	E
C	A	L	L	L	L	L	A	T	E		A	G	E	S
K	T	E	L		E	A	R			E	L	E	C	T
E	R	G		P	I	C	K	K	K	K	K	A	T	Y
T	E	A	R	O	S	E		R	I	G		S	O	L
S	E	L	I	G		A	I	D		E	Y	R	E	
		B	O	S	S	S	S	S	S	T	S			
M	O	S	S		P	T	A			W	A	I	S	T
I	R	E		C	E	Y		P	L	A	I	N	T	S
S	I	X	X	X	X	X	R	A	Y	S		P	O	E
T	O	T	A	L		O	R	R		P	L	O	T	
A	L	E	C		I	O	W	A	A	A	A	A	D	S
K	E	T	T		B	R	E	D		O	N	C	U	E
E	S	S	O		M	O	D	E		K	E	E	P	S

12

	A	H	A	B		V	A	S	T			I	B	I	D
A	G	O	G	O		A	M	O	R			N	O	S	E
G	O	O	E	Y		P	T	U	I			B	L	E	W
A	R	E		O	U	I	S		P	H	O	O	E	Y	
L	A	Y	A	B	E	D			B	L	U	R			
			T	O	Y		G	R	E	E	N	T	E	A	
D	E	W	E	Y		B	L	A	T	S		A	N	T	
O	B	O	E		L	O	U	I	S		S	P	O	T	
E	A	R		W	O	O	E	D		C	H	E	W	Y	
S	Y	M	P	H	O	N	Y			S	H	E			
			R	E	N	E		D	U	E	L	L	E	D	
S	C	R	E	W	Y		B	O	I	L		O	V	A	
U	L	E	E		B	U	O	Y		S	O	O	E	Y	
E	V	A	N		I	D	O	L		E	R	I	N	S	
Y	I	P	S		N	O	P	E		A	B	E	T		

Sixteen answers rhyme: Gooey, Ptui, Louis, etc.

13

D	I	V	A		T	A	T	A		S	T	R	I	P
A	R	A	B		A	D	I	N		P	O	E	T	S
Y	A	L	E		S	A	N	D		I	D	E	S	T
O	N	E	D	I	MAN	MAN	S	I	O	N	A	L		
			N	I	T			R	A	Y				
M	A	R	I	N	A		H	E	E	L		S	O	N
A	L	I	C	E		A	U	T	O		L	O	B	E
D	E	P	A	R	T	MAN	MAN	T	S	T	O	R	E	S
T	R	O	N		I	D	L	E		W	R	E	S	T
V	O	N		S	T	A	Y		P	A	D	R	E	S
			G	N	U			E	I	N				
	G	L	A	S	S	MAN	MAN	A	G	E	R	I	E	
T	R	O	O	P		A	T	A	N		R	A	N	D
B	A	Y	O	U		A	L	T	O		A	S	T	I
S	W	A	M	P		B	E	E	S		S	H	O	E

14

I	L	E			T	H	E	O		O	P	I	E	
C	E	L	L	O		H	A	L	L		F	I	L	M
A	M	A	I	N		A	B	I	D		A	C	L	U
M	O	N	K	👁	D	W	I	T	H		S	T	A	S
E	N	D	E	A	R		B	E	A	R	O	U	T	
			L	R	O	N			T	O	R	R	E	S
W	A	V	Y		M	E	T		S	T	E	A	L	
A	B	A		N	O	W	♡	H	I	S		I	S	A
R	O	L	L	O		S	U	N		I	T	E	M	
P	L	E	A	S	E		D	A	M	N				
	I	N	T	E	N	S	E		L	A	C	A	S	A
A	S	T	I		M	I	D	D	L	🐷	I	G	H	T
C	H	I	N		E	D	G	E		S	T	O	A	T
R	E	N	O		S	L	A	V		T	E	R	R	A
O	D	E	S		H	E	R	O			A	I	R	

15

📦	K	I	T	E		A	P	U		S	H	O	E	📦
C	O	C	O	A		P	E	P		A	M	P	L	E
A	L	E	U	T		E	A	R	E	D	S	E	A	L
R	A	S	P		📦	S	C	O	R	E		R	I	D
			E	E	L		O	A	R		W	A	N	E
I	R	R	E	G	U	L	A	R		H	A	T	E	R
N	E	E		O	N	I	T		M	A	L	I		
📦	O	F	F	I	C	E		B	A	L	L	O	T	📦
		L	U	S	H		B	I	T	S		N	A	E
B	R	E	S	T		P	R	O	C	E	S	S	O	R
R	A	C	E		B	O	O		H	Y	P			
E	M	T		M	U	S	I	C	📦		A	L	O	T
A	S	I	R	E	C	A	L	L		P	R	I	M	O
D	E	V	I	L		D	E	E		E	S	S	A	Y
📦	S	E	A	T		A	R	F		G	E	A	R	📦

16

```
O S T   P E P S I   S C A L P
M A R   A B E A T   E A V E S
E M E R G E N T S   E R I E S
G M V W A N D B M W S U V S
A S I A N     Y E A T S
    N I L S   K O O K I E
S E N D S A N O T E   A N A
U C L A M B A S A N D P H D S
R T E   E X U B E R A N C E
F O R M A L   U R A L
    O L E I C   C A S I O
  G E V C R S A N D H D T V S
P A L E O   B I C A M E R A L
O R B I T   A R O M A   U N I
P R A T T   D O S E S   M A N
```

17

```
J U D G E   S T I N G   S L O
I S E E M   O R D I E   P O P
M A Y [ORG] I U L I A N I   I R E
    E R N I E S   G E [NET] I C
G I F T   I D S   Y E T I
A L L O U T     D U R A N T E
S L A W S   D E A L   G E M
L I M N S   U R L   C A L E B
I N E   P O R E   S N I P E
T I N D E R S   S I N N E R
[COM] E D Y   H E H   A G E S
P A U L I   L A M A R R
I R S   B L A N C H [EDU] B O I S
E L I   L O D G E   C O A S T
D O C   E L Y S E   E R R O L
```

18

```
F A B   T O B E G   A M B L E
R R R   A C E L A   S O L A R
[AU] T O E X H [AU] S T   T W A N G
  R N A   S T E E L E   I D O
G O T T A     S [AU] E R K R [AU] T
L O O   R C A   X E N A
O N S E C O N D   B O O P
B E [AU] J O L A I S N O U V E [AU]
E Y R E   Z O O M L E N S
  C H A R   B R A   R O E
C H [AU] T [AU] Q U A   R A S P S
L A P   G I M L E T   N T H
A D A S H   P [AU] L G [AU] G U I N
S T I L T   U G L I S   F L Y
S O R R Y   S H A F T   F E E
```

19

```
R A M   J U D O   P A S S U P
I C E W A T E R   E T O I L E
M U S I C A L S Y L L [LA] B L E S
S T A L K   O A T S   V E T
    C O C A   L E T H E
A H S O   A M E E R   A R T
D E E   O L A N   A I S H A
D [O] R E MI [FA] S [OL] L A TI [DO] T [IL] A S [OL] F A MI R E [DO]
N A N C E   W E N D   T A G
  T A T   B A S T E   P H D S
  R O W E L   O S L O
T A I   H A U L   U N I T E
S C A L I N G U P A N D [DO] W N
A T N I N E   B A C K S L I D
R A S P E D   E X E S   S T S
```

20

```
G A B O R   C H I P   A R A B
A G R E E   O A T H   M E G R
G E O R G E C L O O   O N L Y
A D A   A S O F   N E S T E A
  D E L T A   M E W   S T N
G R A C I E   L A Y E R
R E X H A R R I S   R E H A B
A V E O   S A M O A   T E L E
Y E S E S   B E N S T I L L E
  S A P I D   S I M P E R
O V A   G A D   K I T E D
R E G I O N   P I S A   E S P
B R A N   F A L L I N G S T A
E N I D   R A U L   I N K E R
D E N Y   Y A M S   C U S P S
```

21

```
F L O O D [H₂O] G A T E  ■  S E A [H₂O]
I R A N I  ■  M O O R  ■  C L E W
R O S E S  ■  A N N E M E A R A
E N T R A N C E S  ■  A N N O Y
[H₂O] ■  E R A  ■  ■  F Y I  ■  ■
W A T E R W A T E R  ■  C H E W
O C A L A  ■  B A S E  ■  S A S H
R U M  ■  Y A C H T E D  ■  S K I
K R I S  ■  S T O A  ■  O C T E T
S A L A  ■  E V E R Y W H E R E
■  ■  M U S  ■  ■  A N E  ■  [H₂O]
H O M E R  ■  P A C H E L B E L
O N I O N R O L L  ■  A S A M I
T E L L  ■  A R G O  ■  S E R I N
[H₂O] B E D  ■  H E A D [H₂O] T A B L E
```

22

```
V I P E R  ■  T U B B  ■  I L L S
E N A T E  ■  O L A Y  ■  M E A L
I N E E D M Y S P A C E
L T D  ■  D E B  ■  S C A L P E D
E W A N  ■  S E T  ■  A M Y  ■
D O S A G E  ■  H E R A  ■  F I E
■  F O R C E D  ■  N S Y N C
N E X T T O N O T H I N G
B Y L A W  ■  A G A T H A  ■
A E S  ■  H U L A  ■  O A R M E N
■  H I S  ■  P R O  ■  K A M A
A R B I T E R  ■  E L I  ■  L B O
L E A V E S O M E R O O M
P A R E  ■  U T N E  ■  D O N D I
O D D S  ■  P U T T  ■  O B E Y S
```

23

```
J E T  ■  S H R U B S  ■  E X P O
A D O  ■  R A I L A T  ■  S H O P
Y G O L O H C Y S P  ■  R O S A
Z E T A  ■  ■  E S S A  ■  U S E R
■  ■  I P O D S  ■  U P C A S T
M S I C A R  ■  E L L I E  ■
R O T  ■  C L A S S  ■  L H A S A
S L E E K E R  ■  A B S T A I N
C O N G A  ■  O F T E N  ■  B A T
■  ■  A G E N T  ■  S E G A M I
O X Y G E N  ■  M A O R I  ■
M E E T  ■  Z O E S  ■  F A C E
B R R R  ■  Y R A N O I T C I D
R O B O  ■  M Y D E A R  ■  H A Y
E X A M  ■  E X E R T S  ■  Y O S
```

24

```
A M I D  ■  S P R E E  ■  A F B S
L A N E  ■  H E A V Y  ■  G I L A
D I S C L A I M E R  ■  R O O F
A M P L E R  ■  P R E S E N C E
■  ■  A N D Y  ■  ■  T E A K S
B U R R S  ■  E M E E R S  ■
A T I E  ■  I S O L D E  ■  I I I
H I D D E N B O D Y P A R T S
A L E  ■  D O U S E S  ■  C R E E
■  ■  M I N T E R  ■  I T S M E
U N W O N  ■  ■  S A D O  ■
N A R R A T E S  ■  R E F O R M
J O I E  ■  E L M E R S G L U E
A M T S  ■  E L E N A  ■  O G E E
M I S O  ■  D A W G S  ■  D A R K
```

The 10 hidden body parts are ARM, EAR, EYE, GUM, HIP, JAW, LEG, LIP, RIB and TOE.

25

```
I T S A F A C T  ■  B A H A M A
L E A P I N T O  ■  E L O P E R
E M P E R O R P E N G U I N S
A P S E  ■  ■  ■  L E A S E T O
■  ■  ■  P I T B O S S  ■  E C O N
C O B  ■  T W I C E  ■  C H E S S
S H O W I E S T  ■  P R O  ■  ■
I M P O S E  ■  ■  L A L A L A
■  ■  U S D  ■  S P A N D R E L
M A R L O  ■  [BLACK/WHITE]  ■  M E G
I R E D  ■  C O Y N E S S  ■  ■
S I M I L A R  ■  ■  O R E O
D A I L Y N E W S P A P E R S
I N T I M E  ■  P E E P H O L E
D E S E E D  ■  A C R O S S E S
```

26

```
I S H   R O C K E T   M C M L
R C A   A T H O M E   I L S A
I R T   S T A R T S   C A T ♀
S E A S H O R E   T S A R
H A R E   ♂ ♀ A N D C H I L D
♀ K I N D   O R A   S A O
    S I R   A N I L   S Y N
  W H E N A ♂ L O V E S A ♀
R A E   N Y S E   E N C
T W A   E L O   E A S T ♂
E A T D R I N K ♂ ♀   N C A A
    S O S O   R U L E S O U T
♂ T E L   T S U R I S   O R E
G O A T   T O P E K A   T U E
O W L S   A B A S E S   S S S
```

27

```
C A P   M U O N S   C H A R
A P U   M E N T A L I M A G E
R O B   R U B B E R N O S E S
E L L   I S A   S E N A T E
E L I   S E R F S   G E E
R O C A   A I R   B O N D
E X T R A B A T T E R Y
D I V I D E D C A P I T A L S
    D E N V E R O M E L E T
I N R E   T I L   S T A R
S I E   L L A M A   E V A
I N C A S H   L E I   R E D
T E A M M A N A G E R   E N D
M A S C A R A C A S E   G E L
E M T S   E M C E E   O D E
```

28

```
A S F A R A S   M A R A C A
M A R S A L A   A D A M A N T
A G A K H A N   S A N T A N A
N A N A S   D R A M   S N A P
A S S N   B A L S A
    T A M A R A   B A N N S
S P A   M A N A   M A S A D A
C A T W A L K   B A C K B A R
A R R A N T   B A M A   S K A
B R A N D   C A S A B A
      A T L A S   S W A G
G A L A   H A S P   P L A T H
A L A S K A N   A T L A N T A
G A S T A N K   R W A N D A N
  S H A N K S   T A N T A R A
```

29

```
P E N P A L   P E P P I L L S
A R O U S E   I L L I N O I S
T O F F E E   C O U N T S O N
C D E F   R O K   C O E N S
H E E P   A F L A S H
    A R T T E S T   P O M P
  M E S A   D N A   I D I O
P I C T U R E P O S T C A R D
E N T R   O R I   S K Y E
A H O Y   L I G H T U P
      P E N S E E   O T R A
R O S I E   F R A   C H A N
A N T E N N A E   M I K A D O
S E A S N A K E   U S E R I D
P I T T Y P A T   P O T P I E
```

30

```
S W I S S   C A B   M O L L S
T E N S E   L E E   E L I O T
R I D E S   A G A   D I N G Y
I G O   T R Y I N G   O G E E
P H O B I A   S P A R S E
S T R O N G   O T C   R R S
    S A S   G L O A T I N G
B O S S   E S E   W E S T
R U T A B A G A   A T A
O R E   B U G   C R I T I C
    A C C E S S   R E N A M E
E L M O   R H I N O S   L P S
S A I N T   E R E   T H E A S
S I N G E   L E X   L E N I N
A R G O T   L E T   E X T R A
```

31

```
MON G E R     G H A N A     S L O WED
I O N E     R E FRI E D     W O O D
C O N S     A R C E D     A C N E
A N A C O N D A     I N R O A D
      I N D       I T E M
S H A N T     U N I V E R S E
W A N D A     E N D O     D E A L
A B E     P U L SAT I N G     F B I
B I A S     P L E A     O P E R A
S T R E S S E D     M A R E S
    D O T S       E E G
D E N A D A     A N D R O P O V
A L O T     G A R Y S     D I D I
T A M E     E N THU S E     A C E R
SUN N E D     S O R E L     S T A TUE
```

32

```
M M M M G O O D     O F F E D
A A A M E M B E R     P R O N E
T E L L S A L I E     T E R R A
T W A     T H A T S T O O B A D
H E R R     A D I O S     N A G S
A S I A N     I E R E     D E E
U T A H A N     S T T E R E S A
      A T O R     S S N S
E X P L O D E S     E N V I E D
X E R     I C E T     A P P L E
P R O B     C H E R I     S A A B
L O T U S E A T E R S     N I E
O X E Y E     L O V E S C E N E
R E G I S     L I O N T A M E R
E D E N S     T R E S P A S S
```

33

```
  R O M     S T I N T     M A T T
V I N N Y     I N A N E     A L O H A
A T A N     S P I N E T I N G L I N G
N I N J A S     G N A T     E K E
E T A     H O W     E R A     R A L
S I N G I N I N T H E R A I N     A G O
    F E T A L       S T A N
B A L E S     M A C     S E E I N G
Y S E R     I N A R U T
H I T     I N T H E B E G I N N I N G
E A T     S R A     I N C A     A B E
A M I N     I A G O     R A M O N
R I N G A D I N G D I N G     N E X T
T O G A E     L E N I N     T I E S
  R O A R     E S S O     E T S
```

34

```
DOG M A     V A M P S     DOG E A T DOG
CAT O N     A B E E T     S P R E E
C R I     CAT O N I N E T A I L S
H A M P E R S     C A L
E L A L     T A R     R R A T E D
R E S O L E     A A U     B I T E
    T O R R I D     CAT S P A W
H U N     CAT S A N D DOG S     S L Y
O H A R E     R I N G U P
T O T O     H E N     I P E C A C
DOG H O U S E     G R E     S O L O
    L A P     A B S O R B S
CAT C H A S CAT C H C A N     N E E
E V A D E     S I E G E     DOG I T
R I D E S     T E R S E     S T S
```

35

```
S L A W     A B E S     C A S T S
H O L E     C O R A     A T H O L
E S A I     E A R N     R E I N A
D E I G N     R O P E R     R E P
      H U N D R E D Y A R D -
U P S I D E S     D I O R
R A I N E D     F R E N C H : Y
S Y M       B R O     E E E
A · I C A L L Y     P A E L L A
    O B O E     S E L F I S H
' N D E R I N C H I E F
N O R     A N D R E     S O F A R
D R O I D     S A K I     R A R A
O S O L E     I V E S     T R E Y
S E L L S     N E L L     S E A S
```

36

E	P	E	E		C	A	R	O	L		P	A	T	S
S	A	R	A		A	C	E	L	A		R	O	A	N
Q	W	E	R	T	Y	U	I	O	P		O	L	I	O
U	N	C	L	E	S		D	R	O	O	P			
E	S	T	E	R		A	S	D	F	G	H	J	K	L
			S	I	L	L			H	E	E	L	S	
D	I	N	S		A	I	D	A		A	T	S	E	A
R	N	A		Z	X	C	V	B	N	M		T	I	T
A	N	G	L	E		E	D	E	N		S	S	N	S
N	I	G	E	R			T	E	S	H				
K	E	Y	B	O	A	R	D	S		P	E	A	R	L
			A	S	S	H	E		S	U	R	R	E	Y
J	O	A	N		T	Y	P	E	W	R	I	T	E	R
A	R	N	O		A	M	O	R	E		F	I	L	E
W	R	E	N		R	E	T	I	E		F	E	S	S

37

P	I	G	L	O	T		P	D	A		A	T	I	T
O	N	E	O	N	E		A	R	C		N	E	M	O
S	T	O	V	E	S		T	U	E		T	E	A	M
T	O	R	E	N	T		R	M	S		I	N	X	S
U	N	G	LOVE	D		R	I	ME		S	C	I		
P	E	E	L		H	E	A	R	S	T		DO	L	E
			O	R	A	N			O	U	T	L	E	T
O	U	T	V	O	T	E		F	U	C	H	S	I	A
A	P	I	E	C	E		E	L	K	E				
F	I	T		C	A	B	L	E	S		BE	A	S	T
		LET	G	O		R	O	D		H	A	S	T	O
H	A	R	E		R	I	T	A		R	A	T	T	A	N
O	L	A	N		B	I	T		A	L	L	U	R	E
P	A	C	E		I	S	H		T	E	E	T	E	R
I	R	K	S		S	H	E		A	S	S	E	S	S

38

(W)	S	E	T		C	R	A	B		W	E	L	L	(S)
T	I	M	E		A	U	R	A		I	D	E	A	L
I	D	E	M		S	T	E	A	K	D	I	A	N	E
D	E	E	P	N	E	S	S		L	E	T	S	A	T
E	A	R	T	H		O	D	E						
		I	L	S	A		R	E	P	R	O	V	E	
A	D	E	N		E	L	B	E		E	A	R	E	D
B	I	G	G	I	R	L	S	D	O	N	T	C	R	Y
B	A	I	L	S		M	A	G	I		T	A	B	S
A	S	S	Y	R	I	A		E	L	A	L			
			S	N	O		H	E	A	T	S			
M	U	S	C	A	T		N	E	G	A	T	I	O	N
I	S	A	A	C	S	T	E	R	N		R	O	B	O
D	E	L	V	E		R	A	G	A		A	L	A	W
(S)	D	A	Y	S		A	L	O	T		P	I	T	(F)

The four corner squares represent Winter, Spring, Summer and Fall.
(The Four Seasons)

39

Z	I	G	S		C	R	E	W		A	B	O	D	E
I	N	A	N		H	E	R	O		S	A	X	O	N
P	O	L	I	T	I	C	A	L	B	E	L	I	E	F
C	R	A	V	A	T		F	R	A	I	D	S	O	
O	O	H	E	D		B	A	S	E		N	A	T	L
D	U	A	L		(S)	A	T		T	H	E	N	O	D
E	T	D		F	E	(L)	L	A		E	S	T	O	S
			N	E	W	S	(A)	N	G	L	E			
G	A	S	E	S		A	N	(N)	U	L		P	A	W
O	B	T	U	S	E		T	O	(T)		S	O	P	H
T	I	E	R		A	W	A	Y		T	E	R	R	A
O	L	E	O	P	R	Y		I	G	E	T	I	T	
P	E	R	S	O	N	A	L	O	P	I	N	I	O	N
O	N	E	I	L		T	O	D	O		T	O	R	O
T	E	R	S	E		T	O	D	D		O	N	I	T

40

A	M	O	R		S	T	R	A	Y		P	I	N	•
P	A	R	E		T	A	U	P	E		O	R	A	L
P	R	E	S	S	U	R	E	•	S		L	A	T	E
T	E	M	P	O			S	T	A	T	E	S		
			O	L	D		P	R	I	O	R	E	S	S
•	O	F	N	O	R	E	T	U	R	N				
E	G	A	D		I	N	A	S		T	R	I	B	E
R	E	C	E	I	P	T		S	P	O	O	N	E	R
S	E	E	D	S		R	E	E	L		C	R	E	E
		N	E	E	D	L	E	•	K	I	T	S		
P	O	T	H	O	L	E	S		A	T	E			
E	R	R	A	T	A			O	T	T	O	S		
S	K	I	S		T	H	R	E	E	•	T	U	R	N
T	I	N	A		E	B	O	N	Y		E	L	S	A
O	N	E	•		D	O	D	G	E		S	L	O	P

• = POINT

41

```
S W E D E   A L F I E   S R I
M I X E D G R E E N S A L A D
O R A N G E M A R M A L A D E
G E M   E N O S   Y U P P I E
      T R E K     E S O S
A S T I R     R I D E S
G H A N A   I S O U R   A M I
R A I N B O W   S H E R B E T
A W L   B J O R K   C H U T E
    D I O N E     T O T E M
C R E W     T V A D
O U T E A T   E R A S   A D O
B L U E B E R R Y M U F F I N
R E D B E A N S A N D R I C E
A D E   D R A I N   S I T E S
```

42

```
* G A M E     D I E T S O D A
B E L I E D   O N C E A D A Y
O N E D G E   N O O N T I M E
X X X I   A T T N   N I N E
      S L I P   M I N
R O A D K I L L   A S Y L U M
I D E M A N D A R E *   E N O
L E I S   E Y E   O T I S
E T O   * E S W I T S W I T H
Y O U N M E   I N A S E N S E
    O A R   T A B S
G U N K   A H S O   S K I M
P E R F E C T *   O N E I D A
E L L E R B E E   S O T T E D
A S S E S S E S   * H E A D
```

*=MATCH

43

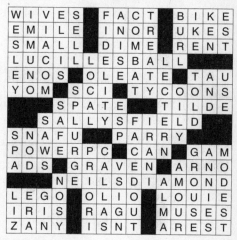

```
W A L S H   A D E P T   R C A
E R A T O   L I N E R   A R I
E L I O T   L A[TENT]P E R I O D
D O N O[TENT]E R   E S S E N C E
    L O D I   S I C S
  N E S T E G G   H A L A S
L O X   N H U   S I L I C A
O N C E B I T[TENT]W I C E S H Y
O N E S E C   A R R   L E S
P O L K A   G I R L I E S
    I T I S   T A O S
C O S M I S M   [TENT]H G R A D E
P A[TENT]O F F I C E   O A R E D
A T O   I O T A S   F E N C E
S S R   C R E P T   F L O O R
```

44

```
W I V E S   F A C T   B I K E
E M I L E   I N O R   U K E S
S M A L L   D I M E   R E N T
L U C I L L E S B A L L
E N O S   O L E A T E   T A U
Y O M   S C I   T Y C O O N S
    S P A T E   T I L D E
    S A L L Y S F I E L D
S N A F U   P A R R Y
P O W E R P C   C A N   G A M
A D S   G R A V E N   A R N O
    N E I L S D I A M O N D
L E G O   O L I O   L O U I E
I R I S   R A G U   M U S E S
Z A N Y   I S N T   A R E S T
```

45

```
S O L O N G   G O T T A R U N
T R I B A L   O K A Y B Y M E
R A M O N A   P I C K I E S T
A T P E A C E   E K E D
T O E   E E R   E B B S
A R R A Y   L O B B Y   E Y E
    L O A   S A Y O N A R A
F A M O U S L A S T W O R D S
A U R E V O I R   E L L
I R E   E N D I T   S O B E R
L A D S   O A K   A V E
    A D D S   S A T I R E S
H A S B E E N S   B I S T R O
I S U R E C A N   O N E A L L
T I M E T O G O   B Y E B Y E
```

46

```
THE   JAI   IMPACT
OILWELL   AREAMAP
YESISEE   MANLESS
    NSC   TSQUARE
PAIGE  TOT   SCI
ANNE  TENET  ENDE
LANDTAX  LOT  DIA
ACETIC    PATIOS
DIR  TIS  NOTMANY
ENCE  TAROT  ONNO
  IVE  TUT  EBSEN
  CROSSAT  ELI
LOCKSIN  BUELLER
ALLEARS  ALGEBRA
TIEDYE  DAY  OAT
```

47

```
CHOP  FONZ    CELS
LINA  ULEES   UFOS
OAST  RATATATTAT
STEROL   LOVE
EATIN  SMOKE   LOU
SLS  ESTATES   EON
    GULAG    ENZO
HAPPYBIRTHDAY
SEMS    CASES
OLE ONDATES   FEW
CLX  KOOLS  STARE
    SECS  SOBERS
DIRTYHARRY  IRAS
EVEL  EGGON  ROTO
NEMO   ESOS  DEAN
```

48

```
EDWARD  QTR  HASP
QUAKER  WYO  ITAL
ULTIMATEPURPOSE
ALTO  WIRETAPPED
LYS  CENT  EGO
  FOR  YAM  SKIP
AUDEN   KHAN  ISR
USINGONESNOODLE
LSD  ONBY  VJDAY
DROP  TAB  SAS
  AVA  OLES  HBO
EXACERBATE  HEAP
ZONINGORDINANCE
RUIN  END  NIMROD
ATNO  TDS  GAMINS
```

49

```
ZESTS  GRABS   GEE
AFTRA  LARUE   OLD
GROUCHOMARX  LIE
SEWN  ORE  BURDEN
  MEDDLING  ARF
   LEDA  ALLRISE
AMIES   SSE   ETS
BENDINGTHERULES
ANA  OOP   ENDTO
BUTTSIN  SWAB
  RAH  GHOULISH
TEABAG  YRS  ALAR
HAN  REVERSESIDE
OTC  INANE  DECAF
USE  FERAL  ODETS
```

50

```
MAMMAL   YESMAAM
ERITREA  ARREARS
SEASTAR  CATNAPS
   IONS  HOAD
ALANIS  ATF  ETC
COLAS  PBS  DROOP
COLI  AID  COSELL
ENE  OCTOPUS  ROE
NIGGLE  MOP  TINA
TERRA  JED  SINES
SOO  TIN  SINGLE
  WORN  THEY
ROADTAX  BARTABS
PRAIRIE  ARRIERE
MARMOTS  IAMSAM
```

51

```
S C A T   A D A M S   A C H E
H A R E   R E B U T   S H O T
I R O N   E L E N A   P A T S
P A S S F A I L C L A S S
S T E E R       H E S   E S S
      S E P I A     S W A T H
A G A   Y E S N O A N S W E R
T U T U   T A T A R   W A V E
O N O F F S W I T C H   Y E W
M I N O R     C H O I R
S T E   A L E       R O L E S
    T R U E F A L S E T E S T
C L I O   A L L A H   A P S O
H A M S   F A T S O   T E E N
E Y E S   S T A T E   E R N E
```

52

```
C A M S   S N A P   R A T O N
O P E C   N A D A   E L E N A
T E R R   O N A N   F E N C E
T E C I R C U M F L E X T E
A K I M B O     U A R
      P I N T I L D E A T A S
A T L   S E A N   S E T O U T
S H U T   O P E   M O R E
O R L E S S   U T A H   L A W
F U U M L A U T H R E R
      A L P     T R I O D E
F A C C E D I L L A A D E S
S L I C K   A M I E   L E I S
H E N C E   T I E S   T O T E
E A T I N   E N D S   O N Y X
```

53

```
A M E N   E S T E S   C A T S
S A L E   C H I M E   A M O I
S Y M B O L I C U N K N O W N
A B E R R A N T   E A R N S
M E R   D I S A S T E R
      A A R   C H A N D L E R
I R A N I   A T O M   O R O
R A T I N G F O R A D U L T S
A G T   R I E N   H A L E Y
Q U A G M I R E   M A W
      R E P E N T E R   U M P
P S H A W   D I A M E T E R
S I M P L E S I G N A T U R E
S L O E   P A N E L   T R I P
T O S S   A N G R Y   A N T S
```

54

```
A S H E   I P A N A   I S L E
S E E K   R O T O R   T O A D
A G R E E K S T O I C S A I D
P O B O X   T Y R O L   P R Y
      U A R       S A M
T H A T M E N S H O U L D B E
H A D     B A T E   S K E I N
I G O   G A R O T T E   L L D
E A R T O   C R U E   H B O
F R E E F R O M P A S S I O N
      D I E       R A N
C P L   S N E A D   G A L A S
H E Y W H A T D O E S Z E N O
A N N A   T E E M S   Z I O N
W A X Y   A S N O T   Y A N G
```

55

```
L I S T S   P I S   R A M S
A N N O Y   A C T   O P I N E
B J O R N F R E E   A R S O N
R U R   C E L I N E D I J O N
A R T S   C A N O N   L U T E
T E S T R U N   S E C   D I A
      O U N C E   R A G E D
  F J O R D E X P L O R E R
V I O L A   T H I N E
E V A   L A G   O P E N I N G
L E N T   C O S T A   A M O R
M O J O S H U P O R K   E T A
A N E Y E   P O P I N J A Y S
S E T O N   T R I   O A S E S
    S T U D   O T C   T R Y T O
```

56

L	O	C	H		T	A	B	O	O		J	O	B	S
I	N	R	E		A	S	I	A	N		E	V	E	R
L	E	A	P		K	I	L	T	S		R	A	R	A
	A	B	C	D	E	F	G	H	I	J	K	L	M	
		A	E	C		E	S	T	A					
F	A	S	T	C	A	R		E	G	R	E	S	S	
O	S	U		R	A	N	G		G	E	N	I	E	
L	F	I	X	L	E	V	I	R	H	Y	O	L	D	M
D	I	T	K	A		E	L	I	E		A	L	I	
S	T	E	E	L	E		N	A	S	T	I	E	S	
		A	N	N	S		D	E	I					
	Z	Y	X	W	V	U	T	S	R	Q	P	O	N	
S	I	A	M		I	R	A	T	E		O	K	E	D
E	T	R	E		E	S	S	E	S		F	R	A	U
M	I	N	N		D	E	I	S	T		F	A	T	E

57

P	A	L	M	E		A	P	E		A	M	A	N
E	L	I	E	L		E	M	I	L		L	I	L	I
A	L	L	A	H		N	A	P	A		A	L	O	E
L	I	L	L	I	A	N	H	E	L	L	M	A	N
E	E	E		P	U	L	L		A	O	N	E	
		M	A	U	I		I	W	O				
W	H	E	E	L		O	N	O		K	E	E	L
W	E	E	W	I	L	L	I	E	W	I	N	K	I	E
W	E	L	L		A	O	L		K	E	E	N	E
		E	M	O		P	H	E	W				
P	H	I	L		K	A	L	E		P	A	L	
H	O	N	O	L	U	L	U	H	A	W	A	I	I
I	O	W	A		A	P	I	N		L	E	M	O	N
A	N	I	L		M	O	N	K		M	A	P	L	E
N	O	E	L		E	N	E		A	L	A	I	N

The answer to 39-Across, when translated by the cipher key at 20- and 55-Across (A=Z, B=Y, C=X, etc.), spells OUR COVER IS BLOWN.

58

C	O	L	A		E	M	I	R		G	A	P	E	S
O	P	A	L		M	I	C	E		E	L	I	Z	A
P	U	B	L	I	C	D	E	F	E	N	D	E	R	S
E	S	S		N	E	S	S		R	I	A	T	A	S
		S	T	E	T		H	O	E	S				
B	A	I	T	E	D		H	I	T	S		O	D	E
O	R	D	E	R		S	A	R	I		A	V	I	S
F	I	L	M	N	O	I	R	A	C	T	R	E	S	S
F	E	E	S		I	T	E	M		S	I	N	C	E
O	L	D		S	L	U	M		S	E	A	S	O	N
		S	E	E	P		H	O	T	S				
A	N	S	W	E	R		P	O	L	S		T	O	E
P	E	T	E	R	S	T	U	Y	V	E	S	A	N	T
E	R	O	D	E		E	R	L	E		E	X	E	C
S	O	W	E	D		N	E	E	D		W	I	S	H

59

V	I	A	L		B	U	M		H	E	A	R	O	F
E	N	L	A	C	I	N	G		A	P	P	E	N	D
T	H	E	G	L	A	S	S	S	L	I	P	P	E	R
T	E	X		A	S	H		O	S	C	A	R		
E	R	I	E	S		E	B	B		S	L	I	E	R
D	E	A	R	S		D	E	E	P		L	E	V	I
		G	A	S		A	R	I	D		V	E	G	
	P	R	O	C	E	S	S	S	E	R	V	E	R	
M	O	I		T	A	C	T		S	E	A			
A	L	O	T		L	A	I	R		S	L	A	D	E
L	O	B	O	S		L	E	I		S	E	V	E	N
		A	R	O	S	E		P	S	I		A	L	T
H	O	M	E	L	E	S	S	S	H	E	L	T	E	R
A	U	B	A	D	E		L	A	U	R	E	A	T	E
G	R	A	T	I	N		O	W	N		T	R	E	E

60

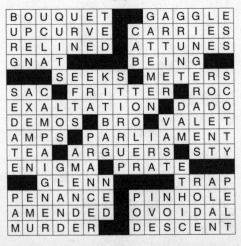

B	O	U	Q	U	E	T		G	A	G	G	L	E
U	P	C	U	R	V	E		C	A	R	R	I	E	S
R	E	L	I	N	E	D		A	T	T	U	N	E	S
G	N	A	T					B	E	I	N	G	
			S	E	E	K	S		M	E	T	E	R	S
S	A	C		F	R	I	T	T	E	R		R	O	C
E	X	A	L	T	A	T	I	O	N		D	A	D	O
D	E	M	O	S		B	R	O		V	A	L	E	T
A	M	P	S		P	A	R	L	I	A	M	E	N	T
T	E	A		A	R	G	U	E	R	S		S	T	Y
E	N	I	G	M	A		P	R	A	T	E		
		G	L	E	N	N			T	R	A	P	
P	E	N	A	N	C	E		P	I	N	H	O	L	E
A	M	E	N	D	E	D		O	V	O	I	D	A	L
M	U	R	D	E	R		D	E	S	C	E	N	T

61

```
S H E B A | C H A D | T O G O
S A L A D | R O T E | A J A R
G R A N D B A H A M A M A M A
T I N D E R B O X | S P I E L
      E D U C | I L S A
C O R D | C A S A B A B A B A
U S E | P E K E | S N A P U P
S H A M U | E L M | T Y P O S
H E R E S Y | M A C E | L Y E
Y A M A H A H A H A | F E S S
      N I T A | O N C E
I N A W E | W A G E L E V E L
L O W E R C A N A D A D A D A
E N O L | D I O N | C O N G O
D O L L | T I N Y | K N E E S
```

62

```
F R A U | B A K E D | C O L E
R E V S | O X I D E | A V I V
E G O S | R E T I E | F A Z E
N A W | I N S E C R E T
C L E A N | T E N A B L E
H E R C U L E S | O N I O N
      E R O S I V E | O N T
  S I D E S P L I T T I N G
U P S | E N A C T E D
R I N G S | S E A L E D U P
I N T E N S E | L A Y T O
      T O P S T O R Y | N E T
M E A L | I T A K E | S A R A
R E D O | F E T I D | S M U T
S L A W | F R I E S | S O S O
```

63

```
E N A T E | F A R O | B A L D
R O L E X | A R A B | A L I E
↑S I D E ↓C A K E | N O V A
T I C S | U T T E R | T E E D
S E I | M N O | O E U V R E
  R A T E D | ↑E N D | E I N
    A R E N A S | S I R E D
B L O C | R E N T A | P A S S
A O R T A | A D O N I S
S O N | G O T↓ | D O O M S
I N A S E C | S E N | O W E
L Y M E | T A K E A | A R E S
I B E X | ↑T O W N ↓B E A T
C I N E | L A N E | E L A T E
A N T S | E N G R | R E U S E
```

64

```
L E A V E | G E T S | S T O W
A L C O A | E X I T | T O R I
G I R L S | L E G O | O U T S
  O V E R S C H L E P P E D
I N S O L E | T E D | E G O
C A T | S A G A S | I B E A M
E P I C | G Y M | E T O
  S C H N A P P S S H O T S
    I O N | L I P | S H A W
A M I N O | B E R R A | I R A
T O N | S T E | I R A N I S
H O C K E Y S C H T I C K
O R A L | S I R E | S C E N T
M E S A | O D O R | E R R O R
E D E N | N E W S | N A S T Y
```

65

```
G E L T | H I S S | T O R S
A R E A | R U R I K | A B E T
G I G I | A M A T I | U L N A
A N S W E R & Q U E S T I O N
      A V E R | R I N G
M A I N E | A S H | P E A C E
O H M | N E T P A Y | S T A R
R E P S | S T O M A | S I L O
E A R P | C L O M P S | O L D
S P E A R | E K E | T E N S E
      S T A S | R E A M
C O S T E L L O & A B B O T T
O B I E | A U R A S | A R I A
P O O R | S T A R T | L E E R
Y E N S | H E L M | M O S S
```

66

```
PIN G  P  O  N  G  ▓  B  O  U  N  D  U  PPIN
S   E  E  S  A  W  S  U  K  R  A  I  N  E
C   O  R  O  N  E  T  M  I  G  H  T  N  T
H   R  H  ▓  A  N  O  D  ▓  N  E  U  T  E  R
E   G  A  N  ▓  S  P  R  I  G  ▓  M  O  R  E
R   I  P  U  P  ▓  S  O  D  ▓  E  V  E
▓   A  S  T  O  R  ▓  P  I  A  ▓  A  D  E
▓   ▓  S  L  E  E  PIN G  B  A  G
▓   C  R  Y  ▓  O  R  G  ▓  E  T  H  I  C
T   H  E  ▓  ▓  O  O  H  ▓  T  A  R  O  T
A   I  N  T  ▓  S  O  F  A  S  ▓  S  O  M  E
I   N  T  O  I  T  ▓  F  R  A  T  ▓  N  P  R
L   O  A  N  E  R  S  ▓  D  R  U  M  M  E  R
S   O  L  A  R  I  A  ▓  C  A  N  T  A  T  A
PIN K  S  L  I  P  S  ▓  H  E  N  N  E  PIN
```

67

```
G  O  S  H  ▓  V  A  R  Y  ▓  F  I  R  M  A
R  A  T  E  ▓  E  R  O  O  ▓  A  S  I  A  N
A  T  O  R  ▓  L  I  L  Y  ▓  R  A  B  I  D
S  E  W  A  R  D  S  F  O  L  L  Y
P  R  E  L  A  T  E  ▓  A  E  S  O  P  S
▓  ▓  D  I  S  N  E  Y  S  F  O  L  L  Y
B  A  B  E  L  ▓  N  E  S  T  ▓  E  I  N
A  W  E  D  ▓  S  A  D  T  O  ▓  B  A  N  C
N  F  L  ▓  M  I  S  O  ▓  B  O  N  K  S
F  U  L  T  O  N  S  F  O  L  L  Y
F  L  Y  I  N  G  ▓  B  O  O  S  T  E  R
▓  G  R  E  A  T  S  U  C  C  E  S  S
V  I  D  E  O  ▓  D  I  E  S  ▓  O  N  T  V
A  D  O  R  E  ▓  E  L  S  E  ▓  U  T  E  P
L  O  E  S  S  ▓  N  E  S  S  ▓  T  O  S  S
```

68

```
B  A  B  A  ▓  F  A  S  T  O  ▓  O  B  O  Y
E  D  I  T  ▓  E  L  L  I  S  ▓  A  R  T  E
A  L  B  S  ▓  R  I  A  N  T  ▓  N  E  O  N
N  I  L  E  ▓  G  E  N  ▓  A  D  D  L  E  S
O  B  E  A  R  I  N  G  ▓  T  I  C
▓  ▓  O  E  R  ▓  R  E  P  H  A  S  E
O  C  O  C  K  ▓  A  D  O  ▓  S  A  L  L  Y
S  A  G  A  ▓  C  E  L  ▓  I  S  E  E
U  S  E  R  S  ▓  E  E  L  ▓  S  N  O  W  O
P  E  E  R  E  S  S  ▓  S  L  O
▓  ▓  Y  E  T  ▓  D  R  O  P  T  H  E  O
C  A  S  T  R  O  ▓  O  O  O  ▓  W  I  N  G
A  N  K  H  ▓  O  K  A  Y  S  ▓  A  N  D  A
A  T  I  E  ▓  P  O  N  C  E  ▓  I  D  E  M
N  E  T  O  ▓  O  P  E  E  N  ▓  N  U  D  E
```

69

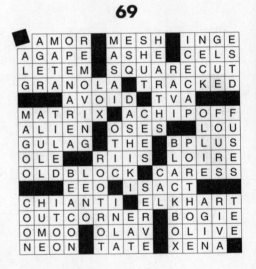

```
▓  A  M  O  R  ▓  M  E  S  H  ▓  I  N  G  E
A  G  A  P  E  ▓  A  S  H  E  ▓  C  E  L  S
L  E  T  E  M  ▓  S  Q  U  A  R  E  C  U  T
G  R  A  N  O  L  A  ▓  T  R  A  C  K  E  D
▓  ▓  A  V  O  I  D  ▓  T  V  A
M  A  T  R  I  X  ▓  A  C  H  I  P  O  F  F
A  L  I  E  N  ▓  O  S  E  S  ▓  L  O  U
G  U  L  A  G  ▓  T  H  E  ▓  B  P  L  U  S
O  L  E  ▓  R  I  I  S  ▓  L  O  I  R  E
O  L  D  B  L  O  C  K  ▓  C  A  R  E  S  S
▓  ▓  E  E  O  ▓  I  S  A  C  T
C  H  I  A  N  T  I  ▓  E  L  K  H  A  R  T
O  U  T  C  O  R  N  E  R  ▓  B  O  G  I  E
O  M  O  O  ▓  O  L  A  V  ▓  O  L  I  V  E
N  E  O  N  ▓  T  A  T  E  ▓  X  E  N  A
```

70

```
O  N  R  Y  E  ▓  S  A  R  A  N  ▓  D  A  B
B  A  C  O  N  ▓  E  L  O  P  E  ▓  I  G  O
S  H  A  K  E  S (P)(E)(A)(R)(E) ▓  L  A  W
▓  ▓  E  M  O  T  E  D  ▓  S  M  A  Z  E
D  U  B  L  I  N  ▓  S  C  O  O  P  E  R
O  S  U  ▓  E  Y  E  S  ▓  A  N  N  I
G  U  L  F  S  ▓  A  T  M  S  ▓  I  D  E  A
M  A  L  L  ▓  F  R  U  I  T  ▓  C  A  R  T
A  L  F (A) ▓  O  L  D  S  ▓  N  A  T (A) L
▓ (I) N  C  A  ▓  Y  O  G  A  ▓ (E) S  A
B  I  G  G  A  M  E  ▓  A  S  I  D  E  S
O  T  H  E  R  ▓  V  A  U  L  T  S
R  A  T  ▓  H  A  I  R  R (A)(I)(S)(I)(N)G
O  L  E  ▓  O  R  L  O  N  ▓  E  U  R  O  S
N  O  R  ▓  P  E  S  O  S  ▓  R  E  A  T  A
```

71

```
S A L E M   A G A R   O P E D
O C A L A   D E L A   B A L I
B E M A D   O T O S C O P E S
    E N O W   O U T R E A C H
A V E   N O O N D A Y
R E X   N O D E   S P I R I T
F C C   A D D S   T R U T H
A T U B           A B R A
R O S E N   S I S I   B I N
F R E E O F   I N O N   E E K
    B R I N G U P   R D S
A G U I L E R A   P R E S
B A R T E R E R S   I V O R Y
E L S A   E N O S   N E L L E
D E A L   S E W N   T R E S S
```

72

```
P A D S   A S S A M   T H D
E L E C   N I T R O   R E I N
A L F A   T R U E R   O H N O
C H I L L I E R W E A T H E R
H E A D Y   M E N U   E D U
E R N   S I E   O R P H A N
S E T S   A N E S   A S S T S
    W I L D G E E S E
S C R A M   S G T S   C A D S
C H U M P S   H S T   N A H
O I D   E A S E   W A C K Y
F L O R I D A V A C A T I O N
F I L A   D R I V E   T E T E
S E P T   L A C E D   I N A S
    S H E   E N T R E   C T N S
```

73

```
I S N O   R E A M S   A R L O
S T A N L E Y C U P   S E E N
E R U T U F E H T O T K C A B
    T I R E S   A R A   T R A
P R I M E R   S T E P S O N S
R A C E S   S H E   P A S S E
O N A   A T E   B E G
    L L A C E R L A T O T
    O P T   B E T   H B O
A S C I I   P E T   S A R A H
C L O S E S E T   L A G E R S
T E M   C C S   C O C O A
I D E J E H T F O N R U T E R
O G R E   M E A T E A T E R S
N E S T   O R D E R   I N A T
```

74

```
D I S C   T E A S E   MELBA
R O M A   E A S E S   N E E D
A N A L G E S I C S   D O NHO
B A L L O N E   E V E N U P
    L I VTY L E R   A L E R T
T I T O   S N A I L
U T O P I A   M I N I   L E T
N E W E N G L A N D S T A T E
E R N   C E E S   S E A S O N
    A R O S E   M T N S
MASHES   S E N T RIES
S T E R E O   T R E N T O N
K A L E   S A V E E N E R G Y
E L E CT   S T I R S   S A L S
D E N S   A M E S S   S W E E
```

75

```
P A L L   T A R A   R A B I N
L E O I   U S E D   E L U D E
A R A M   R E Q D   N O D O Z
T I M B U K T U T U T U
E E Y O R E   I O T A   O C T
    L Y M E   A C T F O R
H A T H   O M A H A H A H A
I N S I G H T   E N R A G E D
T O K Y O Y O Y O   N E N E
I D E A L S   E N D S
T E D   G O A L   E M A J O R
    H O N O L U L U L U L U
S H O U T   R O N A   A R I L
E A R T H   T W I N   M O V E
X H O S A   A S T O   O R E S
```

The New York Times

Crossword Puzzles

The #1 name in crosswords

Available at your local bookstore or online at nytimes.com/nytstore

St. Martin's Griffin